Lesley Blanch, a Londone... part of her life travelling ... books record so vividly. ... she was among the few who advent...d across the USSR, tracing history and literature rather than politics. From 1937–44 she was Features Editor of *Vogue*, 'writing on everything but fashion', as she puts it – theatre, films, books, people. During the war, she also wrote on various aspects of Britain at war for the Ministry of Information.

In 1945 she married Romain Gary, the Russian-born French novelist and Prix Goncourt winner, then an unknown navigator with the Lorraine Squadron of General de Gaulle's Free French Forces. Later, life in the French Diplomatic Service took them from the Balkans to the USA, and they were always off on further travels – Turkey, Central America, North Africa – both writing furiously as they went.

In 1962 their marriage was dissolved. From her base in Paris, Lesley Blanch continued to travel, now east, now west: working a year in Hollywood for the great director George Cukor; crossing Siberia on the legendary Trans-Siberian; in Outer Mongolia, Egypt, Iran and Afghanistan, and returning to the Sahara which inspired her first and celebrated book *The Wilder Shores of Love*.

She now lives on the French Italian border, in a house submerged in tropical greenery, surrounded by the exotica of an exotic life, anchored at last by four adored cats.

A fellow of the Royal Society of Literature, Lesley Blanch is the author of works including the bestselling *The Wilder Shores of Love, The Sabres of Paradise, Under a Lilac-Bleeding Star, The Nine Tiger Man, Journey into the Mind's Eye, Pavilions of the Heart, Pierre Loti: Portrait of an Escapist* and *From Wilder Shores: The Tables of My Travels*.

ROUND THE WORLD
IN
EIGHTY
DISHES

THE WORLD THROUGH
THE KITCHEN WINDOW

For Armchair Travellers
and Enthusiastic Eaters

by

Lesley Blanch

with illustrations by the author

Robin Clark
London

The author
wishes to acknowledge the immortal memory of
Jules Verne's
Round the World in Eighty Days

First published in 1956 by John Murray Limited, London
Published in paperback by Robin Clark Limited 1992
A member of the Namara Group
27/29 Goodge Street
London W1P 1FD

A catalogue record for this book is available from the
British Library

ISBN 0 86072 148 5

Printed and bound in Great Britain
BPCC Hazells Ltd
A Member of BPCC Ltd

Author's Note to this Edition

When I wrote this book nearly forty years ago, people in England were still enduring many post-war restrictions on both travelling and eating. But a benign fate whisked me elsewhere to follow less restricted ways, travelling widely and eating wildly. Thus, to my friends, I became an object of envy or exasperation with every postcard I·sent home. (*Muscat. Supper with pearl divers on their boat. Dashing lot. Shark stew and prickly fig jam for pud. Wish you were here.*)

Today, everyone jets everywhere, a lemming rush to eat everything imaginable and unimaginable, while at home they can obtain dazzling ranges of frozen dishes, so there is little I can add. Nevertheless, I continue to get many requests for this early book, while faithful readers tell me they are still cooking my typical or simplified recipes with gusto.

But before any new readers start flicking over the pages, toying with the idea of making Congo Chicken or Gogel-Mogel, may I remind them *when* those recipes were collected, when those sketches, sketched? Since then, all over the world, political strife, terrorism, famine, television and what is described as progress, have swept away tradition and local colour, replacing them with a remorseless unification or desolation. Were I back in Romania today, I doubt any of the smiling scenes I recalled could still be found. What I wrote of it *then* is cruelly inapplicable now. As elsewhere. . . flora and fauna, open spaces, free seas, are all going, going. Gone.

However, a few traces of traditional ways – mostly by way of the family table – do linger in some places and are cherished, almost defiantly. I hope my readers may still catch glimpses of such colours and flavours through this old book, my kitchen-window peep-show.

Lesley Blanch, 1992

To my mother
Martha Blanch
whose fireside meals I enjoyed more than other
people's banquets

FOREWORD

It is said that a nation is made by what it eats: undoubtedly diet affects character. Lions reared on milky mush cherish lambs. Battles have been determined by indigestion, for we all know that an army marches on its stomach. Walt Whitman, writing of Carlyle, said: 'Dyspepsia is to be traced in every page, and now and then fills the page. . . . *Behind the tally of genius and morals stands the stomach and gives a sort of casting vote.*'

Certain climates produce racial types and characteristics which are expressed individually, by different ways of eating. For example, there is a popular conception that southern food is rich and that southern passions run high. Nothing could be further from the truth. You must go to the north—the dark, ingrown, seething north of Ibsen households—if you want to find overwhelming passions and those rich, nightmare-producing meals which, I feel, may have been responsible for some of Dostoievsky's greatest flights. This north of the Karamazov brothers, of Anna Karenina's ill-fated love, of Gosta Berling's *Atonement*, is the land of *bliini* and *bigos, kouloubiak,* and pickled herrings, sour cream, indigestion and introspection. The Mediterranean, on the contrary, is all lightness—light food, light loves, air, sea, blueness, and dalliance. Everywhere the people are still actuated by a legacy of Greek or Roman classicism—a sense of balance and logic, reflected in many aspects of their daily life, among them their eating habits, which are simple.

> *Lucullus, whom frugality could charm,*
> *Ate roasted turnips at the Sabine farm.*

In this part of the world it is so easy to live well, simply; so easy to love, hate, and love again. . . . Emotions do not smoulder long here. They overboil and are renewed, easily. The sun is a powerful, life-giving force, and a drug, too, seeping that will to suffer which is so obstinately rooted in the north. Passions are soon kindled, soon extinguished in the south. No one broods, and few have indigestion.

If you travel widely, as I have had occasion to do, and look around you at what the various nations eat, and why, and how, you will see that in spite of the apparently injudicious mixtures enjoyed by many other nations few appear (judging by statistics and the prevalence of patent medicines for indigestion) to suffer so much from stomach upsets as the tin-fed Americans and the rather plain-living British, today.

At its best, English food is wonderful: it is more often the cooking which is at fault. My book does not aim to turn you from good English food, but rather to offer you a cook's tour of supplementary dishes—a look at the rest of the world by way of the kitchen table, in the hope that other people's food will spur you to taking even more interest in your own—and, above all, in standards of good cooking. But before I plunge into the international recipes I have collected on my travels, I want to make a few remarks about the place the Ogre Calory has come to occupy in daily life, causing people to fuss over calories before they have learned to *cook*. He seems to have become an omnipresent shade, a far-reaching, globe-trotting kill-joy. Today, in Near Eastern countries, where famine is not unknown, and where ampler curves were once appreciated, dieticians now rear their ugly heads and there are weighing machines peppered about the streets with anxious looking, spellbound peasants climbing on to them over and over again, in the manner of fairground visitors sampling sideshows.

Once, good eating was an end in itself. People ate well, or badly: the rich ate too much and the poor did not have enough: though Dickens speaks of oysters as the poor man's food, so it seems there were compensations. Many people 'exceeded at table', and waist-lines were lost almost as soon as first illusions. But now a shadow falls across the kitchen. A sort of collective dietetic conscience is the spectre at every feast, crying: *Saccharine! Les crudités! No bread! Only* one *potato!*

Once, British and American travellers had only to set foot abroad, on the Continent, that is, to make a series of devout gastronomic pilgrimages, moving from restaurant to *centre gastronomique* with that sleek, glazed-eyed look peculiar to the well-fed. But now, both at home and abroad, they sit calculating their calories (particularly the more figure-conscious Americans) as they consult the menu, juggling their personal weights and measures with that concentration ever associated with the restricted traveller's financial adjustments ('Not soup *and* a sweet . . . coffee is extra').

Therefore, I am prepared to hear many readers mutter uneasily as they turn these pages. Perhaps, eaten exclusively, my recipes might prove enlarging, but not if used, as I suggest, as experimental once-in-a-whilers. I have gone by the old-fashioned standards of what is good and interesting to eat before all else. So come off those scales and get into the kitchen.

Cooking, like eating, is what you make it. For some, a habit; for others, an imaginative art. There are centuries of history, travel, exploration, and adventure behind each dish. All my life I have liked to eat well. I have always been suspicious of those who say, 'I don't care what I eat.' But for many years I was content to enjoy other people's cooking, to take an abstract or theoretic pleasure in restaurant recipes, and to paste-up my discoveries in a gastronomic scrap-book.

Late, far too late, I came to the kitchen, by way of love for a French-Russian husband. I saw myself creating unimagined delicacies. I saw us spending delightful hours together in the kitchen, experimenting, bent over the stove together, flushed with triumph, producing all kinds of classic *plâts* and inventive flights, each contributing some subtle personal touch.

But it has not turned out that way. I, the Briton, never could convert my husband to national delicacies. *Escargots, Tschee, Quiche Lorraine?* He preferred a steak, and infinitely preferred to eat a bun than do any cooking. So I would plough my lonely, fattening furrow, tasting, collecting recipes wherever we went, cooking in all kinds of kitchens and countries.

This book is not a basic cook-book, for most kitchens have one, but rather an appetizer for enthusiastic beginners. In most cases the recipes are simplified or adapted to present means and the possibly unpractised hand that is interested, not so much in preparing an egg dish as such, but one as it is prepared in the Congo, Mexico, or anywhere else.

Today, from the English kitchen of your own home, you can eat your way round the world. With the help of some of the wide range of tinned foods, and the variety of goods now found in the smallest of grocery shops—plus a little ingenuity and enterprise—you can lunch in Turkey or Lapland and dine in Syria. You can try out such strange-sounding dishes as *Foudja djedad, Shashlik, Imam bäildi, Kotletki*, and *Gogel-mogel*.

Not all the dishes I have described are most typical of their country, for, as I said earlier, many are adapted to our present limitations. Even garlic, dill, and wine—three basic ingredients of much Continental cooking—are hard to come by in some parts of England. Still, some of the greatest dishes such as *Poulet Marengo* derived from a desperate shortage, so no doubt lack will act as stimulus to those who really have the chef's instincts.

Without wishing to urge my readers to alcoholic excesses, I suggest they regard water, as such, with suspicion. It ruins many good foods if not kept firmly in its place—which to my mind is the washing-up bowl. *Bubble, bubble, boil and trouble* might be the average English cook's motto. Far too many dishes are boiled into badness. Fish, for example, is excellent poached in cider, instead of water: many meats are best simmered in red wine, or even ale. (Vegetables should almost always be steamed, rather than boiled.) The addition of a little cognac, sherry, marsala, or rum (not rum flavouring) to sauces and many other dishes, is very desirable. However, use discretion; do not make every *plât* a tipsy-cake.

Some of my recipes may seem strange on first reading—but remember, timidity and prejudice should have no place in the kitchen. Imagine what daring it required to be the first to eat a lobster! Remember, too, that if one man's meat is another man's poison, it is only because he allows it to be so. We should not care to eat the puppies considered a delicacy in Tibet; we frown on cannibal cuts; the American predilection for sweet and meat together, bacon with maple syrup, ham and pineapple seems positively morbid to the French, who nevertheless eat apple purée with *boudin*.

I hope my readers will make up their own minds without prejudice or archaic conventions, and enlarge their gastronomic horizons while still within the four walls of home.

CONTENTS

Symbols

B – beverage
D – dessert
E – eggs
F – fish
MISC. – miscellaneous
MF – main course fish

MM – main course meat
MV – main course vegetable
P – poultry
S – salad
SP – soup
V – vegetable

xiii

CONTENTS

SUGGESTIONS FOR BEGINNERS

(We are all beginners each time we do a new dish)

EQUIPMENT

A few pieces of special equipment will make the new dishes easier to cook. Most of these things are found cheaply and easily, if they are not already in your family kitchen.

1. A salad basket, or a colander, to wash and drain vegetables.
2. A flat spatula to lift things without breaking.
3. 2 long-handled wooden spoons (they don't get so hot), and a wooden fork.
4. An apple corer.
5. An egg beater.
6. A vegetable shredder, or chopper; much better than a knife.
7. A big coarse sieve, or strainer, not less than 10 inches across; the kind that looks like a butterfly net, with a handle, is best.
8. Several *big* bowls, so that, in mixing, things don't spill over.
9. One really *big* saucepan, not less than 15 inches across and around 10 inches deep, as well as several others.
10. A double boiler. Two, if possible—one small one for sauces.
11. 1 or 2 casserole dishes, with lids, in earthenware, glass, or enamel, but fireproof, to go in the oven. Large enough for 4 servings.
12. Some little fireproof individual dishes.
13. 1 or 2 asbestos mats, to put on the flame and keep the heat low.
14. A small pastry brush or flat paint-brush.
15. A set of metal skewers.
16. Kitchen scissors, for shredding fine (much easier than a knife).
17. Most important—a measuring cup.

SPECIALLY ABOUT LEMONS

Most dishes are improved by lemon: fish, meat, sweets—it is perhaps the most useful all-round adjunct to the kitchen.

Use the juice

to thin out very sweet jam sauces; squeezed over fish, to give flavour; instead of vinegar, whenever you can; with yoghourt, for a salad dressing; on cut fruits, pears, apples, avocado pears, or bananas, to prevent them from turning dark.

Use the peel

to bring out flavour of meat stews; grated, as a last-minute garnish, for such things as boiled or stewed chicken or duck.

A squeeze of lemon, just before serving, on carrots and most other vegetables and all stewed fruits improves them enormously. AND don't forget that the way to get the most juice out of a lemon is to plunge it into boiling water for 2 or 3 minutes before using.

ABOUT COOKING IN OIL

You will notice that in my recipes I cook a great deal in oil. Oil, or butter; but you can, if you wish, substitute margarine. Personally, I prefer oil for all dishes except those which cry out for butter—the best butter, as the Mad Hatter would say. I never use olive oil, except for a *brandade* (p. 5), finding the taste too heavy, too pronounced. I prefer peanut oil, which is tasteless and light, found easily, or, if not, well worth a little trouble to obtain. Very, very rarely, I use lard—it suits a few dishes, such as Romany Rabbit (p. 11), and I think the best fried bread is made with lard.

A FEW USEFUL TIPS

Put a saucer, or small tin tray or the old lid of a can, beside your stove, so that you can rest on it the spoons or forks with which you are cooking and stirring and do not mess up the stove.

Be sure the kitchen clock is going, or you have a watch, so you can time things exactly.

If you have over-salted a soup, put in one or two cooked potatoes; they will absorb much of the salt flavour.

Before you begin to cook your dish, check the list of all the ingredients you will need, and be sure you have them. (Many a dish has been spoiled by having to rush out, in the middle of cooking, to buy some forgotten thing.)

To flour something evenly, put your flour in a paper bag, drop in the meat or whatever you are flouring a bit at a time, close up the bag tightly, and shake it violently. When you take out the meat, it will be thoroughly covered with flour.

To keep eggs from breaking while they are boiling, put a spoonful of salt in the water, or prick the round end of the shell with a big needle. Always lower the eggs into the water very slowly with a spoon.

To heat cream, usually considered impossible, as it curdles quickly, put 2 large knobs of butter in a small saucepan. Heat the butter till it froths and sizzles. Take it off the flame, pour the cream in, and stir. At once, your cream is hot, and the two substances have blended smoothly.

To skin tomatoes: put them in a pan of boiling water for 1 minute. Then the skin will come off easily. Or you can spear them with a fork, and turn them over the fire for a moment or two.

A vegetable soup—one without any meat at all—is much improved by a lump of sugar cooked with the vegetables.

To keep fish from smelling too fishy while it is being cooked, squeeze the juice of a lemon all over it, both sides, and let it soak in the juice for an hour or so before cooking. Or cook it in a covered dish, in the oven—it will not reek through the house, that way.

Put a dessertspoonful of oil in the water in which you boil rice, and the grains won't stick to the bottom of the saucepan.

To keep cheese fresh and moist, wrap it in a cloth which has been dampened, but not soaked, in vinegar.

When you are peeling onions, you may find they make your eyes water. Hold a bit of bread in your teeth and breathe through your mouth while you work on the onions. Then they won't worry you at all. To take the onion smell off your hands afterwards, wash them at once in *cold* water.

When stirring a thick sauce or anything that is likely to burn or stick to the saucepan, even while you are stirring it, try moving the spoon around as if drawing the figure 8 over and over again across the saucepan. That way, you stir sides and centre too.

If the fat in your frying pan catches fire as it may do, if the flame is too high or the fat spatters overboard, it looks very alarming, for it flames up high. If you try to put it out with water, the water will only push the flame wider. Turn the stove off. Then get salt and throw that on it, and keep on doing it; the flames soon die down and go out.

A Few Extras and Spices for the Cupboard

(most of which can be easily obtained and are necessary for round-the-world cookery)

Allspice, powdered
Anchovy, paste or essence
Bay leaves
Chili powder
Cinnamon, powdered
Cloves, whole and powdered
Curry powder
Dill, dried
Garlic
Ginger, powdered
Mixed herbs, dried
Mace, powdered
Marjoram, dried

Mustard
Nutmeg, powdered or whole
Paprika, sweet
Pearl barley
Rose-water
Rum
Saffron
Sage
Soy sauce (Chinese)
Vanilla extract
Vinegar, tarragon or white wine
Worcester sauce

A Few Special Cooking Terms

(which will help you to understand other cook-books, as well as this one)

To baste
   to spoon hot gravy, or sauce, or any liquid, over the food while it cooks, to prevent it from getting too dry.

To boil
   to continue letting the liquid bubble.

To bring to the boil
to cook until boiling bubbles begin to form on the top.

To marinate
to put something in a specially prepared liquid, and let it soak, from a few hours to overnight.

To parboil
to boil quickly for a few minutes before cooking by some other method.

To reduce
to boil a gravy, or sugar, or sauce, very fast over great heat until it begins to boil away. As it does so, it grows less in quantity but stronger in flavour, sometimes thicker.

To sauté
to brown quickly and lightly in a little fat.

To seal, or sear
to put food (usually meat) into a very hot oven, or to cook it for a few minutes on a hot fire, so that the outside is sealed, keeping all the goodness, the juices and flavour inside. This should never take more than about 5–10 minutes. After which you cook the meat slowly.

To simmer
to cook something very, very slowly, on the lowest possible heat, so that it keeps just at low boiling point, but never boils over. (An asbestos mat is helpful here.)

PRINCIPAL WEIGHTS AND MEASURES

A pinch or a dash	equals less than half a saltspoon
3 teaspoons	equal 1 tablespoon
2 breakfast cups of granulated sugar	equal 1 pound
2 breakfast cups of butter (or fat)	equal 1 pound
2 breakfast cups of chopped meat	equal 1 pound
2 breakfast cups of liquid	equal 1 pint
4 breakfast cups of flour	equal 1 pound
4 breakfast cups of liquid	equal 1 quart
4 quarts (or 16 breakfast cups) of liquid	equal 1 gallon

NOTE ON WEIGHTS AND MEASURES AND OVEN-HEAT

You will find that I do not give you the quantities in measures of
ounces, pints, or pounds, except for buying amounts. This is because,
in my own experience of cooking I find it much easier to know the
quantities by spoons and cups. It has often happened to me that I
am in a kitchen where there is no measuring cup, no scales . . . in
fact, in most of the foreign kitchens and faraway places where I have
watched other people cooking, these things are never seen. (Imagine
Turkish peasants or Finnish hunters with scales!) Then, too, other
countries measure by grammes, or litres, just as they use centimetres,
instead of inches. So, it always seems better, to me, to use spoons
and cups—or even the eye, to measure by.

This deliberate inexactitude applies to oven-heat too. I have not
given precise temperature figures for there are so many different
kinds of cookers that I am giving you only the bare indications—
very hot—medium—or low. You will soon arrive at working this
out on your own kind of stove.

Learning to cook is mostly by seeing, by *doing it*; like anything else,
you learn as you go along. You will very soon find out *about* how much
(about is a very useful word in cooking) flour you need to mix with
a cup of water, to get the thickness or thinness you want. The best
way to learn is to start in and try. Most cooks will tell you they
don't know *exactly* the quantities they use of this and the other . . .
'*about* a cup of that . . . *about* 10 minutes' boiling . . .' Cooking is
like everything else. You have to find out for yourself.

EUROPE

PAIN PERDU (Lost Bread : from France)   (for 6)
  (*In England this dish is called The Poor Knights of Windsor*)

The French nation is celebrated all over the world for its wonderful
food. It is true that every country has some special dish, but perhaps
the French have more than any other. In any case, they are all
deeply interested in good cooking, take a lot of trouble over even
the simplest everyday food, and care passionately what they eat.
'Serious' is an adjective often applied to gastronomy. '*Une maison
serieuse*' they say of a restaurant they recommend: or, of a woman
who cooks really well—'*une femme serieuse.*' Praise could go no higher.
The celebrated French chef, Monsieur Vatel, stabbed himself to death
when the fish did not arrive in time for a dinner in honour of Louis
XIV. But it is just this fact, that they do take so much trouble over the
simplest food, that makes the French such famous cooks; it is far more
how they cook than *what* they cook that has made them celebrated.

I have chosen here some of the simplest dishes; but prepared with
a lot of care and attention, they have become famous all over the
world. *Pain Perdu*, for example, is eaten throughout France as a
favourite dessert. It is, in fact, a variation of bread and butter
pudding, though rather more elegant. I first learned to make it,
along with several other good French dishes, when our house in the
Midi was swarming with village builders who were taking their own
time in repairing its crumbling walls. Although the Midi is not,
strictly speaking *un centre gastronomique* like Strasbourg or Lyons, I
always noticed the builders were deeply interested in food, and
during their two hours mid-day break they would sit in the shade
under the olives, swigging red wine and discussing the merits of one
kind of *saucisson* or another. They never left the house without
saying *Bon Appetit!*, and sometimes they would come into the kitchen,
lifting saucepan lids, advising and discussing my efforts most know-
ledgeably. After a heated argument with the foreman over the
respective merits of *tchak-tchouka* and *ratatouille* (both simmered
vegetables, one from Tunis, the other from Provence) I found I
was treated with a new warmth. The mason was heard to remark to
the plumber that *some* English cared what they eat: and when the

3

carpenter built new shelves for my modest *batterie de cuisine* he said '*Tiens!* Madame does not content herself with sandwiches, then?'

After that, it was one long, delightful *causerie gastronomique*. Advice was lavished on me. Elaborate and unpronounceable regional foods were described to me in the bewildering local patois. Out of all the confusion, came such pleasures as *Panisse*, *Pain Bagnia*, and *Pain Perdu*, too.

And once, on a day of overpowering heat, before we had achieved a refrigerator, and when our larder was bare, five unexpected guests descended, all very vivacious, and sat about, getting increasingly glum as they waited to be fed. Tiptoeing to the back door, I confided in the builders, who took over completely. Mario brought in a neighbour's chicken and started plucking it, while Cæsar fetched vegetables from his own *terre* as they call their little allotment gardens. These are often a mile or so beyond the village, where they all live huddled in gardenless houses behind the medieval fortress walls. Marcel, the foreman, clumped into the kitchen to show me how to make *Pain Perdu*—a dish he had often described lyrically, but which I had dismissed as too much trouble.

I shall always remember him, far too large for the kitchen, covered in cement splashes, his huge paws delicately beating eggs and measuring sugar. No doubt he made life unbearable for his wife in her own kitchen; no doubt he was then the one sitting about glumly waiting to be fed. But in my kitchen he was the hero who saved the day and taught me how to make *Pain Perdu*. Here it is:

6 slices stale white bread	3 egg yolks
¾ cup milk	2 tablespoons butter
1 tablespoon sugar	Cinnamon
¼ teaspoon vanilla extract	

Take 6 slices stale white bread about ½ inch thick. Remove crusts. Bring to a boil ¾ cup milk with 1 tablespoon sugar and ¼ teaspoon vanilla extract. Pour the milk into a soup plate or flat dish. Cool a little and dip the slices of bread in it. Dip them fast, in and out, so they do not become soggy or break, and lay them on a plate to drain, while you beat up the yolks of 3 eggs. Put these in another soup plate, and dip your slices of bread in the egg mixture, carefully but quickly, so that each side gets evenly eggy. Use a spatula to handle them. Put them to drain on a clean cloth, or a big sheet of paper for a moment or two. Now melt some butter—for 6 slices about 2 table-spoons—in a frying pan. When it starts to smoke, that is the moment to fry the slices very quickly, first one side, then the other. When they are a *pale* golden brown they are done. Sprinkle them with sugar and cinnamon and serve them piled up and wrapped in a clean napkin to keep them warm. 'The dish is none the worse for it, and it looks genteel', as one old cook-book says.

BRANDADE OF CODFISH (from Brittany)   (for 4)

This takes rather a long time to prepare, but it is superlatively good, particularly as made in Brittany, where the fishermen and their families, living in those austere white-washed villages along the savage, rocky coastline, live largely on fish. Fresh or salted cod spells dullness to me, unless it is transformed, as in a *brandade*. Personally, when young, I grew to loathe codfish, for we were served nauseous hunks of it at school; and, later, much of my life seems to have been spent cooking cods' heads for my many cats. In retrospect I see myself, like the daughter of Herodias, always confronted by a re-proachful head on a platter.

But *brandade* banishes all such memories. Here codfish undergoes a magical change, and steps up into the class of *pâté*, and can very well be the *pièce de résistance* for a party. There are several variations of *brandade*. Catherine, my Basque cook, at once a tower of strength and an emotional tempest in the kitchen, advocates the Provençal, no-milk way, but I prefer the Breton way. This is how to make it:

1½ pounds codfish, salted or dried	1 cup milk
4 or 5 cloves of garlic	1 cup olive oil
	Salt and black pepper

Take 1½ pounds salted, or dried, codfish, and let it soak all night in cold water to cover. Next day drain the fish, bring it to a boil in fresh water, and let simmer. After 5 minutes it should be cooked

5

tender. Drain again, cut it in small pieces, removing all the bones and skin. Mash in a lot of garlic. No good making a *brandade* if you don't like garlic, for this needs a lot of it. Use about 4 to 5 garlic cloves, peeled, chopped small, and then crushed, or mashed, into the fish. Warm 1 cup milk in a small saucepan. In another saucepan heat 1 cup salad oil (olive oil is best). Keep them on a *very* low fire; they must not boil. It is best, once they are warm, just to stand them near the fire, not on it. Now add alternate spoonfuls, first one of milk, then one of oil, to the fish, stirring 1 or 2 minutes between each addition. The stirring and mashing is best done with a wooden spoon.

When all the milk and oil are gone, and you are positively worn out with stirring, your *brandade* should be ready, a lovely, thick, smooth *purée*, looking like mashed potatoes. Add pepper and salt (it should be highly seasoned). You can eat it hot or cold. If hot, then warm it up thoroughly in a saucepan, over a low flame, and serve with quarters of lemon and perhaps little triangles of fried bread (see p. xviii). If served cold, it is best with dry toast.

GREEN SALAD (from France)   (for 4)

You may wonder why I write about salads in a cookery book. But a green salad is one of the 'musts' with every French meal, in every province, a sort of signature to any French menu, so perhaps something about how to make the best kind is appropriate here. The classic French one is about the best I know. While in America they overdress their salads, in England salad is generally underdressed to the point of nudity, and apt to be interpreted as large wet lettuce leaves with perhaps some beetroot, all floating in water and vinegar, and thus unfit for man or rabbit. The French, great classicists, frown on the American habit of secreting unlikely substances in their salads, cubes of cream cheese, tinned fruit, or dollops of jam, but I am not surprised. When I was in the States these large bowls of mystery seemed to assume the proportion of some unlucky dip;

whatever you fished up was bound to be wrong—from the point of view of the classic salad, that is. In France, a salad is always eaten as a course by itself, sometimes with cheese, but after, never with, the main dish. It is usually of plain lettuce, sometimes of endive, or *mâche* (lamb's lettuce, or field salad), or else chicory, but that is about all. Sometimes tomatoes are added, beetroot never. Mayonnaise is not used for this plain green salad but it is reserved for special kinds, such as potato salad. An oil and vinegar, or lemon, dressing is usual, and the bowl is well rubbed with garlic. Now here is the way to make a really good French salad.

1 head lettuce or 4 heads chicory or 1 head endive
Garlic (optional)
3 tablespoons peanut oil or olive oil
1 tablespoon lemon juice or tarragon vinegar or light white wine vinegar
½ teaspoon salt
Pepper to taste
¼ teaspoon dry mustard (optional)
¼ teaspoon sugar
2 tablespoons chopped spring onions (optional)
2 tablespoons parsley (optional)
2 tablespoons fresh dill (optional)

1. Mix the salad in a bowl really large enough to be able to turn it easily without pieces falling overboard. For 4 people, you'd be surprised what a large bowl you need.

2. Be sure your salad leaves have been well washed and are really well dried. You will never get a good salad if water remains in. Shake your wet lettuce several times, swinging it round and round in a salad basket, or, if you haven't one, a clean cloth. Now let it drain and dry in the air for 10 minutes. Shake it again in a dry cloth. It should be crisp, fresh, yet quite dry.

3. Rub your bowl with a piece of garlic if you like the flavour. It improves a salad greatly.

4. Mix your dressing: for 1 head of lettuce, enough for 4 people, put in 3 tablespoons oil. (I find peanut oil the lightest and best for salads, and it does not have that very strong taste which some

people find disagreeable in olive oil.) Add 1 tablespoon lemon juice or tarragon vinegar or light white wine vinegar; add nearly ½ teaspoon salt, a big shake of pepper, ¼ teaspoon dry mustard or not, as you like, and ¼ teaspoon sugar. Mix all this into your oil and vinegar and stir well. Pour into the salad bowl.

5. Put in half your salad leaves and turn them thoroughly till they are all well covered with the dressing. Then put in the other half and continue turning it lightly, but thoroughly. Don't mash it, or the leaves will be sodden. Just keep turning lightly, over and over. To finish, you can sprinkle with fine-chopped spring onions, the green stalk part, about 2 tablespoons; or fine-chopped parsley; or better still, fresh dill, chopped fine. This gives a most delicate, delicious flavour.

I know all this sounds a long troublesome process, but it is well worth it. Once you have mastered this art—for so the French consider it—you will find most people want to eat your salad in preference to any other.

ROQUEBRUNE TARTINE (from Provence)   (for 4)

This is properly known as *Pain Bagnia*, a speciality of the lovely coast between Mentone and Marseilles; but as we eat it a great deal in my home village of Roquebrune, among the olives and cypress groves hanging high above the Mediterranean and the little harbour of Monaco, I call it *Roquebrune Tartine*. It is very simple to make; a perfect picnic food. Indeed, I don't know what we should do without it in Roquebrune, for the hazards of housekeeping there are considerable. So many feast-days or Saints' days are announced by the clanging of the church bell, Grande Margharita as it is called locally, and then within an hour or so, the few shops empty, and the grocer, the butcher and the baker go out to celebrate, to drink their wine and to play boule at the vine-shaded bowling ground. Far below, you may glimpse a few tiny cockle-shell boats in the bay. Maybe—but only maybe— a fisherman will climb up to the village, through the terraced groves of olives, bringing his catch. His arrival is announced by a handbell and clapper, at which everyone who

wants some fish (and all the cats of the village) rushes to the Place des Deux Frères. Sometimes the rival fish-merchant turns up too. She is rising eighty, and usually gets a lift up the hill in the municipal dust-cart, her basket balanced on the mound of garbage, so that I, for one, do not patronize her. Thus, as you see, housekeeping can be a chancy affair and *Roquebrune Tartine* is a great stand-by.

1 loaf long French bread or 4 French rolls	Few cooked green string beans (optional)
Garlic	3 or 4 anchovies
10 stoned ripe olives	2 tablespoons olive oil
1 red pimento	1 teaspoon lemon juice or vinegar
2 tomatoes	

Get a long French loaf, or 4 French rolls, cut them in half, length-wise. Rub cut surfaces with garlic. Spread them with a mash of the following: 10 stoned ripe olives, 1 sliced red pimento, 2 small tomatoes, and a few strips of green string beans if you have them. Some people add 3 or 4 anchovies, but they have a very strong taste, so be cautious. Mix everything together with about 2 tablespoons olive oil, and 1 teaspoon vinegar or lemon juice. When the mixture has become nice and smooth, spread it thickly over the bread. Now put the 2 halves of your loaf or rolls back together, and either tie round with string, or put them under a pastry board or tray with something heavy on top. Leave them to settle down a bit—say an hour at least. Then they are ready. Perfect picnic food.

VEAL MARENGO (from France)   (for 6)

Napoleon said that an army marched on its stomach: he himself was not a great gourmet, only insisting on a roast chicken, *on the instant*, whenever he called for it. This necessitated a complicated arrangement by which a series of birds were always roasting, in relays, the clock round. Napoleon's generals, however, appear to have taken the question of cuisine very seriously, and we find that at least one culinary classic derives from the Napoleonic campaigns. Mayonnaise takes its name from a later general, MacMahon, who, when bivouacked in some devastated village during the Crimean campaign was told the fish could have no sauce, there was nothing left but some oil and a few eggs. 'Then look sharp and make a sauce with them', was his reply; and thus came the sublime mayonnaise (mahonnaise) we know today. Similarly, after the Battle of Marengo, Napoleon and his staff, cold, tired, and hungry, found themselves separated from their supply wagons. The one cook who was with them had nothing for supper but chickens and nothing to cook with them but some tomatoes. He made what turned out to be a culinary masterpiece by cooking the chickens in oil with cognac, and making a sauce of tomatoes. It sounds simple, but I daresay the brandy added a very special flavour. Since then dishes with a preponderance of tomato flavouring are often loosely dubbed 'Marengo'. Here, then, is *Veal Marengo* (without brandy, however).

3–4 pounds veal rump	Salt and pepper
½ cup olive oil	1 cup water
2 tablespoons butter	3 tablespoons tomato purée
1 large onion	Pinch of dried mixed herbs
3 tablespoons flour	½ pound mushrooms

For 6 people, take 3 to 4 pounds veal rump—cut in 1½ inch cubes. Put ½ cup olive oil and 2 tablespoons butter into a big frying pan or any dish you can heat over the flame. Put your veal into this and cook rather fast, turning frequently till it becomes a reddish colour. This should take about 10 minutes. Peel and cut thin 1 big onion. Add this to the meat and cook till it is a pale golden brown. Sprinkle meat and onion with 3 tablespoons flour, salt, and pepper to taste, and stir gently. Stir in 1 cup water, 3 tablespoons tomato purée, and a pinch of dried mixed herbs. Stir gently; if meat is not quite covered by the sauce add a little more water and tomato purée. Put the lid on and leave this to simmer very gently for 1 hour over the asbestos mat. Meanwhile, wash, peel, and remove stems from about ½ pound mushrooms (tinned ones, if no others are available). Slice very thin. Stir into the veal and tomato and simmer another 15 minutes. At the last moment, stir in 3 tablespoons double cream (and if you can, a little cognac or marsala).

ROMANY RABBIT (from any Gypsy Camp) (for 4)

The Gypsies, or Romany people, are a proud, ancient race, and anyone who writes of them as 'gypsies', with a small G is no friend of mine. They are as much a people, with their own traditions, history, language, and customs as any other. Yet they do not have any one country, being found in most countries, part of, yet quite apart from all the rest of the inhabitants, going from town to town, selling the baskets and cradles they make, doing a bit of tinkering—mending copper and tin—and, I fear, often a bit of poaching, too. They pick up a pheasant, or any bird they can catch, on any of the land they pass. Rabbits are their more usual fare. Anyway, they have always been eating rabbit stew whenever they have been so kind as to ask me to eat with them.

I love the Gypsy people, and have looked for them wherever I have been, though I never saw any in Switzerland. I have seen them in the most unexpected places such as one New Year's Eve in New York, at Grand Central Station, of all places, where they were dancing a sort of fandango, between trains. The Gypsies of France are centred at Les Saintes Maries, in a desolate prairie country called the Carmargue, at the mouth of the river Rhône. It is a flat, strange land, where they raise a particularly fine breed of black bulls and the herdsmen ride white horses. Here the Gypsies come from all over the world, once a year, to make a pilgrimage to their own church.

In Bulgaria the Gypsies lived in curious mud-hut encampments, where the huts were hardly high enough for a child to enter; these settlements were called *mahallas*. Toward the Turkish frontier they lived in caves eaten out of the limestone cliffs. In Roumania and Hungary they wandered from village to village, their dancing bears lumbering after them, and their shaggy horses pulling carts full of rough sheepskins, tambourines and violins, and a few kettles and pots and pans, their only possessions. In Roumania they were the wildest creatures I have ever seen anywhere. When they played their violins it was the most seductive music imaginable, and I used to wish it would never stop.

I do not think they are very interested in food—fortunately—for they often go short. They live off the land, wherever they may be, and seldom have money to buy the cheeses, sugars, spices, jams, and milk which more settled people use regularly. They eat a rabbit stew, some berries, or any fruit or vegetable they find (they never stay anywhere long enough to own a garden or grow vegetables for themselves), and bake a rough sort of bread, perhaps, and drink a brew of herb tea. Bacon—which means getting a pig and curing it themselves—is regarded as a great rarity, but I remember one excellent rabbit and bacon stew I ate with some Gypsies in Cornwall, long ago. They made it in the simplest possible way, as you could do it, if you were in camp, or at a particularly elaborate picnic.

1 rabbit	Lemon peel
Oil	1 turnip
4 cups water	4 sticks celery
½ cup raisins	2 tomatoes
Salt and pepper	Mixed dried herbs
4 onions	Pinch sage
4 carrots	3 or 4 slices bacon
1 clove garlic	4–8 potatoes
3 sprigs parsley	½ tin tomato soup
2 or 3 cloves	

The skinned rabbit, cut in pieces, is first browned in a frying pan with a little oil or bacon fat. Then put it in a saucepan, cover with 4 cups water, add ½ cup raisins, salt and pepper, 4 onions, chopped, 4 carrots cut in rounds, 1 clove garlic, 3 sprigs parsley, 2 or 3 cloves, 2 or 3 pieces of lemon peel, a small turnip peeled and cut in chunks, 4 sticks of celery, 2 tomatoes cut up, a sprinkle of mixed dried herbs, and a pinch of sage, 3 or 4 slices bacon, and 4–8 potatoes peeled and cut in half. All this is very slowly stewed (with a lid on the pot of course), for at least 2 hours. If the liquid seems to be boiling away, I think you should cheat: that is, do not add water, but rather ½ tin tomato soup. Of course this was not done by the Gypsies, but it would be a good idea if you had a tin of soup handy.

After this dish I think some rather strong cheese and watercress and wafer biscuits or brown bread would be good and, although not strictly on the Gypsies' menu, still very much in their tradition.

GUARD'S PUDDING (from England) (for 4)

English food is often most unjustly reviled, but only by those who have never sampled its masterpieces. Best of all, and sometimes mentioned to me in awed tones by foreigners in faraway places—the English pudding: the glorious, sustaining, uninhibited pudding, frankly based on suet. It seems to be rather out of favour just now,

when the more ethereal jellies are said to be as nourishing (though *no one* could say as good) and less fattening. The Ogre Calory has spoken: Suet settles on the hips. Well, it is welcome to settle on mine, for one, and no cook-book I write shall ignore the delights of one or other of these spurned English classics.

Looking back, I seem to remember puddings for every occasion and person. Christmas Pudding, Guard's Pudding, Roly-Poly Pudding, Canary Pudding, Spotted Dog, Apple Hat, Bird's Nest

Pudding, Castle Pudding, Seven-Cup, Empress, St. Leonard's, Bachelor's, Admiral's, Friar's, Nun's, and Marble Pudding. . . . (Could that one be on the heavy side? No matter.) In retrospect, the faraway pudding-eating England of my infancy seems to have been an endless procession of these solid joys constructed and demolished, day after day; always followed by the ritualistic outing to walk it off. And in the late winter's afternoon twilight we used to go homewards, if possible following the old lamp-lighter on his rounds. He carried a long pole with a light on top, and at each street lamp he stopped, touched the lamp with the stick, at which it lit, magically. In a few old-fashioned London streets this practice still continues, and when I return from my travels and see the lamp-lighter again, I am overcome by a wave of nostalgia—not so much for the safe world of my childhood, as for suet puddings.

So back to cooking—puddings especially. One outstanding sweet is (traditionally) served to the Guards Officers on duty at Whitehall or St. James's Palace. Lucky creatures; no wonder they all look so pleased with themselves. Here is the recipe for Guard's Pudding, which, as it happens, is guiltless of suet—but sustaining enough, for all that.

1 cup white breadcrumbs	Thin cream (optional)
¾ cup sugar	or
¾ cup butter	3 extra tablespoons raspberry
Pinch of baking soda	jam for sauce
3 eggs	2 tablespoons water
6 tablespoons raspberry jam	Juice of ½ lemon

Mix 1 cup white breadcrumbs with ¾ cup sugar and ¾ cup butter. Add a pinch of baking soda dissolved in 1 teaspoon water. Next, beat up 3 eggs thoroughly, and add 6 tablespoons good raspberry jam. Mix the whole thing together vigorously. Put it all into a mould or pudding dish that you have first buttered. Steam it for 2 hours. To do this, stand the mould in a double boiler or a saucepan of boiling water, but be sure the water doesn't come more than halfway up the sides of the mould. No lid on the saucepan, of course, and you must keep an eye on it to see that the water does not all boil away. From time to time, add a little more, to keep it always at the same level. This pudding is served with either light cream, or a thin sauce made of some more jam: 3 big spoonfuls of jam and 2 of water, boiled together a minute or so. At the last moment add the juice of ½ lemon, and stir well.

FRUIT HAT (from England) (for 4)

Here is another succulent pudding from England: but this time one that is very easy to make. Sometimes it is called Summer Pudding, since it can be done with several kinds of fruits.

8 or more thick slices white bread	½ cup sugar (minimum)
2 cups fresh blackcurrants, raspberries, or blackberries	Cream or milk (optional)

Cut 8 slices of white bread (no crusts) and line the inside of a pudding-basin with them: put the slices very close, so that no cracks are left between. Now fill it up, packed tight, with 2 cups fresh black-currants, raspberries, or blackberries, very lightly stewed: press them down hard, so that their juice runs out and soaks the bread. Sugar plentifully as you are putting in the fruit. Finish by covering with more sliced bread, and put on top of the dish a flat lid or a plate that fits tight onto, and *into* it. Then put a weight on it, an iron, a heavy tin, or whatever you can find, so that the lid is pressed down. Leave it all night in the refrigerator. Next day, gently loosen the pudding on the sides with a knife. Put your serving dish upside down on top of it, hold it and the pudding-basin firmly together, and turn them over so that the pudding comes out neatly on the serving dish. It will stand up, splendid and firm, like a strange sort of hat. It will have become a deep purply-red, and all the juice will be soaked into the bread. It would not be perhaps a very becoming hat to wear, but it is wonderful to eat, which I think is really better. Cream makes an agreeable trimming to this sort of hat.

STEAK AND KIDNEY PUDDING (for 4)

Since I have made no secret of my *faiblesse* for suet puddings, and they are generally rather out of fashion today, it may not be amiss to include one recipe, even for the English reader. I have chosen a steak and kidney pudding, as this is usually held to be less heavy than precisely the same pudding served as a sweet. Here, then, is this majestic mixture—England's birthright.

$\frac{1}{2}$ pound flour   1 pound stewing steak
$\frac{1}{4}$ pound shredded suet $\frac{1}{2}$ pound beef kidney
Salt and pepper

To make the suet crust, mix shredded suet, flour, salt, and pepper, with enough cold water to knead into a stiff dough. Roll out as if for pastry, and line a pudding basin with the dough, leaving aside enough to form a lid. Cut steak and kidney into small chunks; put it into a paper bag containing 4 tablespoons flour, and salt and pepper. Shake it round vigorously then put the meat into the lined pudding basin, and add 1 cup cold water. Be sure the contents fill up the basin (that is, do not choose too large a pudding basin), so that when you put on the dough or suet crust lid, it is well supported.

Cover the top with greaseproof paper, and tie it round, under the rim of the basin, with string or rubber band. Now tie the whole thing up in a clean cloth (leaving the knot on top, by which you can handle the bundle). Put your tied-up pudding into a big saucepan ¼ full of boiling water. Boil the pudding for at least 3 hours. From time to time, look at it, and if the water is boiled away, replenish with more boiling (not cold) water. To serve, take it out by its top-knot, remove this cloth, and wrap the basin in a fresh one (the other will have become a bit suety). Stand the lordly whole on a dish —'and send it away hot', as an old-fashioned cook used to say, with a wave of her hand to indicate those remote, upper regions to which she dispatched her chef d'oeuvre.

EEL SOUP (from Holland)   (for 4)

Eel is the hot-dog of Holland. Everyone eats and loves it. You can
buy it from little carts in the street. Smoked eel is as delicate and
delicious as smoked trout, but it is a *very* rich dish. Eel soup is as
satisfying and less overpowering. The pieces of fish are eaten with
the soup. Add boiled potatoes and you have a solid meal.

This is the sort of dish that seems to belong to the Dutch painters,
Vermeer, or Gerard Douw; the world of quiet tiled kitchens where
huge rosy women prepare vegetables and fish, and outside we
glimpse the still, lemon glow of twilight across the steeply gabled
red roofs. It is a prim world, where, surprisingly, great bursts of
gusty lewd laughter and the gargantuan oyster feasts of Jan Steen
have a place, too: where guitar players strum to riotous groups of
wine-bibbers, and overturned roasts are gulped by sly little pet dogs.

1 pound eel	$\frac{1}{4}$ teaspoon powdered mace
4 cups salted water	2 tablespoons butter
6 sprigs parsley	2 tablespoons flour
2 teaspoons capers	Dash of black pepper
Peel of $\frac{1}{2}$ lemon	

For 4 people, get 1 pound eel from the fishmonger, and have it
cleaned, skinned, and cut into 2-inch pieces. Put it in a big saucepan with 4 cups salted water. Simmer till the fish is cooked, about
$\frac{1}{2}$ hour. Lift the pieces out and put them aside in a warm place.
To the water they were cooked in add 6 sprigs of parsley, 2 teaspoons
capers, the peel of $\frac{1}{2}$ lemon, and $\frac{1}{4}$ teaspoon powdered mace. Melt
2 tablespoons butter and blend with 2 tablespoons flour and cook
till it is creamy. Add this to the fish stock and stir well. When it
begins to thicken let it simmer (asbestos mat), for 15 minutes.
Sprinkle with a dash of black pepper, and pour it through a strainer
(so capers and parsley and lemon peel do not get in) over your pieces
of eel. Reheat for a few minutes if the eel is not really hot. Serve with
mashed or boiled potatoes.

FLEMISH ASPARAGUS   (for 4)

Here is a good way to eat asparagus and to enjoy to the very last the delicious melted butter which should always accompany it, in my opinion. The thrifty Belgian families I knew in Bruges used to serve it this way, in little dark, orderly dining-rooms that looked out over the canal, tree-shaded, calm, green, and still.

2½ pounds fresh asparagus	¼ pound butter
3 egg yolks, hard-boiled	Salt and pepper

Soak 2½ pounds fresh asparagus in cold water to remove sand and earth (about 15 minutes). Plunge in boiling slightly salted water, and cook for about 12–15 minutes, if young; 20–25 minutes, if old. Be sure your pan is large enough to hold the asparagus without breaking the tips. (Which, by the way, cook quicker than the stalks, so some people cook the asparagus standing up, tips out of the water. If the pot is tightly covered, the tips steam done while the stalks are boiling tender.) They are easier to handle if you tie them in little bundles, one bundle per portion. Prepare the sauce to serve with them by first hard-boiling 3 eggs; mash the yolks very fine. Now melt about ¼ pound butter, cut in pieces, and when it is melted and very hot, add it, bit by bit, to the egg mash. A smooth, creamy yellow sauce will be the result. Add a little pepper and salt; serve at once, in a well-warmed pot or jug. You will find it is delicious and easier to finish, to the last delicious drop, than plain butter, which is apt to trickle about the plate in a watery way, and go to waste sadly.

BELGIAN CUCUMBER (from Flanders)   (for 4)
(You can do chicory the same way, too)

It is easy to imagine the people of the Low Countries to be placid: and by comparison with the more volatile French, the Belgians and Walloons seem phlegmatic. Yet I recall violent events in a small hotel in the Lowlands.

The chef, whose thunderous black-browed good looks spoke of the Spanish ancestry common to many in this part of Flanders, was passionately enamoured of a coquettish miss who waited at table. Her engaging ways endeared her to many of the visitors—in particular to a florid, prosperous cognac salesman from Bordeaux who made frequent visits to the hotel. On these occasions, the chef made a habit of leaving the kitchen hatch open, even when he was not passing dishes through. We became accustomed to seeing his darkling glance following Josette from table to table. 'This will finish badly,' said my companion, who enjoyed other people's dramas as much as his own. One memorable evening, as we watched Josette encouraging the brandy merchant's gallantry, the hatch was suddenly flung open and a large carving knife flashed over our heads to land, quivering in the wall beside Josette. All was uproar! Chairs overturned, trays crashed to the ground, Madame, who supervised the *caisse*, began to scream, and continued, on one piercing monotonous note. The knife was followed by a meat cleaver, equally ineffectually aimed, before the chef was dragged away glaring and unrepentant. Josette, quite mistress of the situation, pouted and shrugged and preened, but the cognac merchant bawled for his bill and left on the instant, and has never been back since. Madame sacked Josette next day. But the chef was kept—he was too good a cook to lose for a little upset. And I must admit that when things had quietened down and we got our dinner, the way he served cucumber was particularly delicious, and not in the least indigestible, by the way. Cooked, it loses all its dangers, while keeping its subtle flavour.

For Recipe Turn the Page

4 medium cucumbers   Mayonnaise (optional)
1 egg yolk   Fresh dill, chopped
1 pot yoghourt

Peel 4 medium cucumbers, cut them in thick rounds, each one about 3 inches long. Poach them in boiling water (covered), with a dash of salt, for 10 minutes, or a little less, till tender. Drain well and put the cucumbers in a flat fireproof dish. Make a sauce of 1 yolk of egg, beaten with a pot of yoghourt (or even some ready-made mayonnaise mixed with the yoghourt). Warm but don't boil this, spread it over the cucumber, and sprinkle with fresh chopped dill if possible. This is refreshing on a summer's evening; have it as a main dish: with brown bread; and cheese and fruit to follow.

Or you can serve cucumbers pickled the Polish way (ready prepared, from the delicatessen shop).

6 medium dill pickles   Grated cheese
White sauce (see page 169)   Butter

Take about 6 medium-sized dill pickles. Arrange them in a casserole dish. Make a simple white sauce and pour this over them. Sprinkle thickly with grated cheese and dabs of butter, and cook in a medium hot oven for 15 minutes. This is not a sustaining main course, but it would be very good to begin a meal with, or to enliven cold meat. And while we are on the subject of vegetables, you might try carrots cooked with raisins. Cook the carrots in water, to which you have added a handful of raisins. To serve, drain off the water, reheat the vegetables with a large knob of butter and a dessert spoonful of sugar, so that it browns, or 'caramelizes' a little. I used to eat carrots cooked this way at Dinant, the prim little town that borders the Meuse, where the glassy still water reflects every house and spire, and where they specialize in making a special sort of gingerbread. . . . I bought a set of saints, and arranged them along a shelf in my kitchen, where they stayed for years, staled into rock-like hardness, and having the appearance of carved wood. Unsuspecting visitors always took them for curious pieces of medieval sculpture. I never disillusioned them.

TOMATO ICE (party food from Luxembourg)   (for 4)

St. Honoré is the patron saint of pastry-cooks: I think his head-quarters must be Luxembourg, famous for its cakes. I recall patisserie shops where people came to eat a whole meal, entirely of different sorts of pastries, marrons glacés, chocolate éclairs, coffee creams, fruit tarts, rhum babas, all sorts of fantasies, chocolate-cream logs, with a marzipan bark, icing sugar swans and delightful little cakes called *religieuses*. It was before anyone counted calories, and the cakes were accompanied by a rather sweet glass of white wine, or a cup of chocolate with whipped cream. I imagine the 'calory intake' as those who are scientific about their weight, call it, would amount to hundreds of thousands: but I know I enjoyed myself madly, wandering from one counter to another, with a little tray and a pair of tongs with which to lift up the pastries I was amassing steadily.

One night, at a dinner-party, when the mere thought of any more to eat made me feel wan, I remember an astute hostess tempted even my jaded appetite with something I had never eaten before—a tomato ice. It is an excellent dish to round off a sustaining dinner, especially for those sophisticates who don't admit to a liking for sweet things. Here is the recipe I was given.

1 cup mayonnaise	Garlic, crushed
½ cup sour cream	Juice of ½ onion
Salt and pepper	Cucumber, sliced
1 cup fresh tomato juice (or ½ cup tinned tomato juice or purée)	Pretzels or pretzel sticks (optional)

Mix mayonnaise (ready-made will do) with ½ cup sour cream, plenty of salt and pepper, 1 cup fresh tomato juice or ½ cup of the tinned kind, a few very, very small specks of crushed garlic, and a little onion juice. (Press half an onion in a squeezer.) Mix all this up thoroughly, and put in an ice tray or other dish in the freezing compartment till firm. Serve surrounded by thin slices of cucumber and hot cheese biscuits. An outer ring of pretzels looks well and tastes right with this. Anyhow, it will be something very special, if you make it right.

FONDUE (from Switzerland)   (for 4)

When I lived in Switzerland, I must admit that those very qualities
of security, quiet, and cleanliness which are so much vaunted, and
attract so many visitors were those which I found least pleasing. It

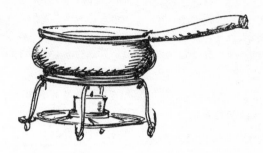

was like living in a world of mechanical-toy efficiency, the orderly
procession of hours punctuated by cuckoo-clock chimes. During my
two years there, I made several journeys to the Sahara, however, and
a more violent difference could not be imagined. Yet as I wandered
blissfully about Southern Algeria, becalmed in sand and silence, in a
latitude where there seems to be no time, only space, I used, even
in that torrid, haphazard land to feel, at times, a twinge of longing
for a good Swiss *fondue*. 'Never the time and the place, and the loved
one, all together', says the proverb; if only I could have sat under
the date palms of El Golea, sharing a *fondue*, or a *raclette* (another
cheese dish) with my Arab friends. But there it was—or rather, there
was I, being offered the eternal green tea and dates from which my
hosts brushed the flies with tender solicitude while I watched the
Chaamba (a desert tribe who form the core of a special military
camel corps) feeding their *mehari*, or fast camels, with grain which
they placed in the hood of their outspread burnous, so that no sand
should get in. Some of these warriors were adopting the coaxing tone
of anxious mothers wheedling difficult children to eat nourishing
food. And the camels, their long serpent-like necks stretched, their
supercilious glances ranging from man to food, grunted and groaned
and seemed bored with their menu. What was Switzerland like,
asked the Arabs? No sandstorms? No flies? Cold? (No colder than

parts of the Sahara at nightfall). Snow? A lot of water? Yes. And fountains, fantastic gilded fountains everywhere. . . . Tourists by the thousand, too. Very different from El Golea . . . and yet, people sitting round the fire there, too. But in scrubbed kitchens or pin neat inns. No camels tethered outside. No Ouled Nàil dancing girls, either, with their jangling gold-coin jewellery, their serpentine arms and undulating bellies. An accordion solo and a yodelling song or two, maybe, and of course, the *fondue*, the desirable, delicious *fondue* which I crave, wherever I am. This is how to make one.

2 tablespoons butter	1 pound Gruyère cheese
3 tablespoons flour	Salt and pepper
2 cups milk	$\frac{1}{2}$ teaspoon grated nutmeg

To make this dish classically, you should have dry white wine and a small glass of Kirsch in place of milk, and you should have a chafing dish, or one of those little stands in which a candle burns, so that you can make it at the table on very slow heat, stirring it every moment, and it is served there and then, piping hot. Of course you can do this on the stove, but it's not such fun, and it's much harder to keep the heat as low as it should be to do a real *fondue*. Let us suppose you are cooking it at table: light your little light, warm your earthenware casserole dish, which rests on the stand over the flame, as I have drawn. Melt 2 tablespoons butter in it. Add 3 tablespoons flour, stirring carefully, round and round, with a wooden spoon. Now add, bit by bit, always stirring, 2 cups milk. When the milk and flour mixture begins to thicken a little, add 1 pound coarsely grated or shredded Gruyère cheese. Buy it in a lump and cut it into thin shavings yourself. Stir all the while. Never leave it alone. Now your cheese has melted. Add salt and pepper, and about $\frac{1}{2}$ teaspoon grated nutmeg.

By now your *fondue* is ready. The Swiss tradition is to eat it this way: the dish is in the middle of the table; the guests, each armed with a plateful of white bread cut in cubes about 2 inches square, all dip their bread in the *fondue*, spearing the squares on a fork. The person who first loses a chunk of bread, letting it fall into the *fondue*, has to stand the rest of the table a new bottle of white wine, the traditional drink with this dish.

ROCOCO CREAM (from Austria)   (for 4)

Austria has the reputation for good food: and Gerard de Nerval described Vienna as the dining-room of Europe: though I have not found the food exceptional there, except for their very rich, frothy desserts and pastries, and great dollops of whipped cream on top of their coffee or chocolate. This ornamentation is called *Schlagober*. The richness of the food always reminds me of the traditional curlicue architecture found in the houses and churches of Vienna, Innsbruck, Salzburg, and all the old towns. This seventeenth and eighteenth century style, baroque and rococo, is pretty, fussy, rich, and gay. The houses are pink or yellow, or pale green, like cakes. Most of them have fancy white decorations that seem to be made of cream, instead of plaster or wood. Most churches are just as fancy. Inside, they are a mass of gold, pale bright colours and painted frescoes, and the statues of saints are dressed in laces and velvets and wear jewelled crowns, and seem to look down with a worldly, blasé air.

Salzburg is the town where Mozart was born and lived as an infant prodigy, composing his sublime music, so that all the world came to marvel at him before he was eight. His house still stands there, a tall, narrow house in a narrow street full of houses decorated like pastries. Above the roofs you can see the whipped-cream peaks of the Salzkammergut. And the dozens of cafés are still full of people talking about music, about Mozart's music in particular, and the Mozart Festival held there each summer. Everyone drinks coffee with Schlagober on top. When they have dinner it is usually a dish of veal, or pork and sauerkraut, with caraway seeds and lots of potatoes. And perhaps, the chocolate cream, or mousse, which I will now tell you how to make.

$\frac{1}{4}$ pound semi-sweet chocolate	$1\frac{1}{2}$ tablespoons vanilla
2 tablespoons hot water	Icing sugar
4 eggs, separated	Whipped cream
	Raw coffee

Take $\frac{1}{4}$ pound semi-sweet chocolate and break it into small pieces or use chocolate chips. Melt the chocolate in a small saucepan over a very low flame with 2 tablespoons hot water, stirring carefully all the time. Beat the yolks of 4 eggs and $1\frac{1}{2}$ tablespoons vanilla extract. Whip the whites of the 4 eggs very stiff. Mix the whole thing, whites, yolks, and chocolate, gently together. Then spoon it into small cups or individual pots. Put them in the refrigerator, or leave to cool. Serve one to each person, topped with plenty of whipped cream, and a light sprinkling of raw coffee—the coarse-ground crunchy sort.

POTSDAM PORK CHOPS (from Germany) (for 4)

A lot of German food seems heavy to us. The Germans like solid dishes, dumplings, all sorts of sausages, rich dishes of goose and sauerkraut, and various meats cooked in beer. I find them very soporific. This dish of pork chops is not so heavy. It used to be the speciality of an inn near the gates of the palace at Potsdam, where I remember going to see the gardens and the beautiful little palace built by Frederick the Great as a copy of one at Versailles, for he passionately admired everything French. Here he used to entertain Voltaire, and other French luminaries. They used to dine in a round dining-room overlooking the flight of steps leading down toward the park below, and beyond it the little town of Potsdam. I believe Frederick the Great liked French food too; but he probably offered his distinguished guest typical German dishes. Perhaps something on these lines would have given a local flavour to the Frenchified whole.

4 large loin pork chops	2 cups bouillon (or stock)
12 dried prunes (or 1 jar baby-food prunes)	6 or 8 small onions
	$\frac{1}{2}$ big white cabbage
Salt and pepper	6 cloves
Oil	1 tablespoon flour

For 4 people, take 4 large loin pork chops. Lightly cook about 12 dried prunes in water till they are soft. Remove the stones and pound the prunes to a pulp. (Or you can use a jar of baby-food prunes—already cooked and mashed.) Spread this on one side of the chops, and add plenty of salt and pepper. Put 2 of the chops face to face, the prune mixture inside, like a sandwich. Tie them together. Then do the same with the other 2. Put them in a hot frying pan with a little oil, and lightly brown each side. Transfer to a casserole, add 2 cups bouillon or stock, 6 or 8 small onions (first browned in oil), and $\frac{1}{2}$ a white cabbage, shredded. Add 6 cloves, salt and pepper. Put a lid on the casserole and let it cook very slowly in the oven for an hour and a half. When cooked, cut the strings and place your pork chops on a dish, side by side. Surround with the cabbage and onions. Mix a tablespoon of flour with a little of the sauce; add mustard, salt, and pepper. When it is smooth add it to the rest of the sauce in the casserole and stir until it thickens. Pour this over the chops. Serve with mashed potatoes.

CHEESE MUFF (from Bavaria)   (for 2)

To me, Bavaria is always dominated by the personality of the mad King Ludwig, who revelled in complications—in living, in architecture, even in cooking. *Hechtenkraut* was the favourite dish of this unhappy monarch, whom, however, we have in part to thank for Wagner's glorious music, for it was he who rescued the composer from a life of poverty and neglect and built an opera house where his music could be heard and enjoyed. Ludwig was very neurotic and did not like to meet people. He used to sleep all day, and get up at

31

sunset, when he took breakfast. His lunch was at midnight, and his supper at dawn. His servants found this topsy-turvy timetable hard, especially as the King seldom stayed long in any of the splendid palaces he was always building, all over his mountain kingdom. He would decide to drive to one of them, and at once the gilded sleigh would be prepared, the white horses harnessed with their scarlet ostrich-plume decorations, and the King would set off in the middle of the night, driving through the snowy forests, preceded by a galloping line of cooks and servants racing to reach the palace before him and to have all in readiness. *Hechtenkraut* (casserole of pike and cabbage and crayfish) was a dish the King liked to eat after such a sleigh ride. But it must have been tough on the cooks.

When I was staying near Bayreuth for the Wagner Festival, plunged into a limbo-land of emotion, gorged on Wagnerian splendours, we used to drive home through the woods, drunk with sound, stunned with the violent Wagnerian impact and no doubt quite unfit to be in charge of a car. Sometimes, descending from the immortal heights we would feel the need for mere earthly sustenance (though nothing so complicated as *Hechtenkraut*), and, oh! weakness of the flesh, stop at some wayside inn to eat sausages. Sometimes we used to order a cheese dish, known, I think, as Cheese Muff. It was as rich and indigestible a mixture as Wagner's music. They say cooked cheese produces nightmares, but we always slept perfectly afterwards. Perhaps we were still lulled by Tristan's divine Liebestod.

¼ pound Cheddar or Gruyère cheese	½ cup white breadcrumbs
4 tablespoons butter	2 eggs
	Salt and pepper

Here is Bavarian Cheese Muff. (One eats little of this, for it is very rich.) Grate ¼ pound of cheese (about a cupful). Melt 4 tablespoons butter in a saucepan over a low flame. Add ½ cup white breadcrumbs and the grated cheese, and stir it well (wooden spoon, please) until it is melted. Add 2 well-beaten eggs, salt, and pepper. Stir all the while, and as soon as the mixture begins to form into a soft, fluffy, muff like shape, it is done. Serve at once, with toast, or dry biscuits. A very plain salad, after this, with a tiny bit of oil and lemon dressing. The Muff is on the heavy side, so don't add a creamy dessert. Fruit, coffee, maybe—nothing more.

TARHONYIA GOULASH (from Hungary)   (for 4)

The Hungarians love very highly flavoured foods, with lots of fiery red peppers and paprika. This seems to go with their love of vivid, and traditional clothes, the scarlet and purple and emerald flowered handkerchiefs the peasant women tie over their heads, and their stiff-pleated crimson or flower-printed skirts, once with as many as twenty starched white lace petticoats underneath, and worn, surprisingly, with high, shiny black boots, to which they sometimes attach little metal heel-plates which clink as they move: they are known as 'musical heels' among the Magyars. The men wear huge shaggy sheepskin-lined coats, or bright red, braid-trimmed jackets flung over one shoulder, and little black bowler hats trimmed with bouquets of flowers and ribbons and worn tipped forward in the

33

manner now adopted by so many fashion-conscious Englishmen. A village festival looks toyshop-like with dolls all dancing the *csárdás* or the polka, or singing, or riding the wild horses they breed on the Putza, the great central plains of Hungary.

Goulash is the national dish. This is best eaten in the winter, and it takes nearly all day to cook (by itself, mostly, so it is worth while remembering that it can be prepared and then left quite safely). Sometimes it is accompanied by *Tarhonyia*, a sort of home-made pâte, of flour and water, cut into little chips, and baked hard, before being cooked in water, like spaghetti. *Tarhonyia* is not easy to make. I suggest pearl barley as a substitute. Here is one version of goulash:

2 pounds lean beef	2 bay leaves
½ cup flour	4 big dried prunes
¼ teaspoon salt	1 clove garlic
Black pepper	1 teaspoon sweet paprika
2 tablespoons oil	2 cups water or red wine
4 onions, chopped	2 tablespoons cream
4 tomatoes	(optional)
2 tablespoons pearl barley	

Take 2 pounds lean beef and cut it into squares about 2 inches thick. Put ½ cup flour into a clean paper bag, with ¼ teaspoon salt, and plenty of pepper. Now put in the meat, shut the bag tightly, and shake it vigorously a few times, till evenly floured. Brown it quickly in a frying pan with 2 tablespoons oil and 4 chopped onions. Choose a casserole with a tight cover in earthenware, cast iron, or glassware. Put the meat and onions in, with 4 tomatoes cut in quarters, 2 tablespoons pearl barley (instead of *Tarhonyia*), 2 bay leaves, 4 big dried prunes, 1 clove garlic, chopped up small, and 1 teaspoon paprika (the gentle, sweet paprika, of course, unless you want the roof of your mouth to feel skinned). Pour 2 cups water over the mixture. Or use red wine, the cheapest possible kind will do.

Now put the cover on tight, and put the casserole in a medium hot oven. After 20 minutes, turn the oven lower, as low as you can, and leave the goulash alone for 4 or 5 hours at least. About half time look at it and stir it gently. If it is getting dry, add about ½ cup more of the liquid you are using, but only a little at a time, and only if it looks thirsty, so to speak. Don't drown it, or it won't thicken up again, but don't let it get at all dried up: there should be plenty of gravy. The longer, the more slowly it cooks, the better it will be.

If you want to be very fancy, stir in a couple of tablespoons of cream just before you bring the dish to table, but don't do this until the last moment, for if the cream cooks in the oven it will curdle. Serve potatoes baked in their jackets with this goulash.

THE GOLEM'S DUMPLINGS (from Czechoslovakia)   (for 2)

The Golem is a legendary creature said to have existed in medieval Prague, the capital of Czechoslovakia, or, as it was then, Bohemia. Prague is full of narrow streets that wind their way up to the pointed turrets of the Hradchin Castle high on its hill, overlooking the river. The old part of the town is full of dark mysterious legends. I remember the Street of the Alchemists, where you felt that if you could peer into the tiny windows you would see necromancers and magicians and witches, all mixing magic draughts and casting spells. The legend of the Golem belongs here. It was said to be a giant creature created by the Rabbi Judah Löw, a sort of robot, or mechanical man, who could walk and work but not think or feel. It was set to work in the house, but at last it became so powerful that everyone was terrified of what it would do next. As it had been brought to life, or action, by some magic signs, 'the Shem', which were written on a piece of paper and put into its mouth, it was only destroyed when the Rabbi Löw chased it through the streets, and finally managed to get 'the Shem' out of its mouth. At this point, it fell to dust at his feet and never troubled the people of Prague again. Some rags of its clothing were preserved in the old Synagogue, where I was shown what was supposed to have been the Golem's coat.

In any case, the Golem remains a legend of old Prague, and people still remember it. No one could ever tell me if the Golem ate or drank like a living being, but if he did, I am sure he would have drunk beer, the Pilsner beer which is made at Pilsen, not far from Prague, and eaten dumplings, which are one of the Czech's favourite dishes. They can be eaten with meat or jam; or in soup, or with caraway seeds inside. This is how to make the dumplings.

6 tablespoons flour	1 tin clear soup (not packet)
Pinch of salt	or 4 cups water
3 eggs, separated	Grated cheese (optional)
2 tablespoons butter	1 tablespoon caraway seeds
	(optional)

Put 6 tablespoons flour into a big bowl, with a pinch of salt. Beat the yolks of 3 eggs and mix in 2 tablespoons soft butter. Cream all this together, eggs, butter, and flour. Work the dough very smooth.

A wooden spoon is best. Beat the whites of the eggs very stiff and add to the mixture. Stir hard for another minute or two. Shape the dough into small round balls (do this with your hands, of course). They can be any size you like: small tangerine size, I would suggest. Now drop them into a saucepan full of boiling stock (clear soup) or water. When the dumplings rise and float on the surface, they are done. If you are going to eat them with jam, of course you don't want to poach them in soup, but in water only. If you cook them in a tinned soup, such as beef or chicken consommé, then you might serve soup and dumplings with a little grated cheese, and it would make a most sustaining winter's meal. If you want to add caraway seeds to your dumplings, sprinkle them into your dough when you are mixing it.

KOTLETKI (from Poland) (for 4)

Polish people eat a lot of fish, and of course, being mostly Roman Catholics, they eat it on Fridays and fast days and on Christmas Eve, too, when stuffed carp is the traditional dish. (Another tradition of this night is that some straw must be spread under the tablecloth, in memory of the Manger.)

A simpler Polish dish that can be made with either fresh or tinned salmon is *Kotletki* which we should call rissoles, probably. Variations on this theme are found in many countries. In Greece, made with meat, beans, and local flavourings, they are called *Kephtedes*. In Turkey, made with rice and olives and vine leaves, and heavy with oil, they are *Soutsouka*. This is Polish *Kotletki*.

1 cup white bread	1 pinch of pepper
½ cup milk	1 teaspoon nutmeg
½ pound tinned salmon (or	Flour
fresh salmon cooked with	Butter
1 sliced onion)	Cucumber
4 tablespoons butter	Yoghourt
2 pinches of salt	

Take a cup of white bread, broken into small pieces (no crust), and soak this in ½ cup milk. When it is nice and soft, mix it with ½ pound of the best tinned salmon, well drained and broken up with a fork. (If you want to use fresh salmon instead of tinned, simmer the fish gently in water to cover, with 1 sliced onion and a little salt for 15 minutes, remove from water and let cool.) Beat bread and salmon together with 4 tablespoons melted butter. Add salt and pepper, 2 pinches of salt and 1 of pepper, and then—this is the secret of making this taste specially good—sprinkle *plenty* of nutmeg into the mixture, at least 1 teaspoon, and again mix it all well. Now shape this sticky mass into little thick sausages about 4 inches long, flour them lightly, and sauté in butter or oil. Serve with them, as a vegetable, thin slices of raw cucumber and a bowl of yoghourt for a sauce.

It is these additions which lift the dish out of banality into exoticism, so don't make *Kotletki* unless you have the extras to hand.

CAFÉ KAUNAS   (for 4)

This is also called Café Polonaise, but as I first drank it in a small café in Kaunas, in what was then Lithuania, I remember it this way: a small dark inn, ornamented inside by a majestic, enormous white porcelain stove which hummed and sizzled cosily. Outside, an elaborate gilded iron sign hanging from the steeply tiled roof, a curly dragon eating a pretzel I think it was: but that part of the world has a whole animal and monster kingdom of such beasts curling and twining round the shop-signs, holding lanterns in their mouths, or serving as rain-spouts. Inside the café a number of citizens were drinking glasses of tea, *à la Russe*, or this heady brew, the Café Kaunas I am going to tell you about. Most of them were reading the newspapers provided by the café, each fixed to a curious sort of cane frame enabling them to be held open in one hand, leaving the other free for the cup, or for waving about with that vehemence associated with central European political discussions.

I used to make this brew myself in London during the war, when with all our shortages, we were never without coffee or cocoa. It used to round off a rather bleak meal, giving the illusion of sugary plenty. Don't try it though, if you don't have a sweet tooth.

3 tea cups strong black coffee   1 cup very strong chocolate
Sugar   or cocoa (or a bar of
                                    unsweetened chocolate)

When you have strained your coffee, pour it into a jug: add the chocolate or cocoa (I prefer cocoa) beaten to a froth; add sugar to taste, and beat the whole together, briskly. Reheat and serve at once. For this, I use sugar from a separate sugar canister in which I keep a stick of vanilla—but that is just an elegant extra. The Café Kaunas should be thickish. If you make it by grating chocolate, be sure it is thoroughly melted by mixing it first, bit by bit, with the hot coffee. And you must adjust your quantity of sugar to whether your cocoa or chocolate is sweetened, or otherwise.

KIECIEL (from Poland)   (for 4)

This is a typical Slav dessert. You can make it with many different fruit juices. Cherry, redcurrant, raspberry, or strawberry juice are best. You can make it with the extra juice left from tinned or stewed fruit, too.

2 cups fruit juice   1 tablespoon cornflour
Sugar, to taste

Strain the juice—let us say, 2 cups. Mix a tablespoon of cornflour with a little of the juice, stirring until it is smooth and free of
lumps. Then add the rest of the juice and sugar to taste.

Now put all of this into a saucepan, and bring it to the boil slowly,
stirring constantly so that it does not burn. When the mixture starts
to thicken, pour it into a mould and leave it to set. If you can leave
it all night, all the better. Leave it in the refrigerator, but don't put
it in until it has cooled off. If it is properly firm, you can turn it out,
like a jelly. But if it remains a little wobbly, then give it a last quick
whip so that it is like a thick purée, and serve it that way; sour cream
or milk are good with it, and a sweet biscuit, too.

GOGEL-MOGEL (from the Ukraine)   (for 2)

I don't know why this exquisite, rich golden sweet is called *Gogel-
mogel*. Russian children have always loved it, and eaten it for
special treat days, birthdays and festivals. To me, it sounds like the
name of one of those fairy creatures, gnomes, witches, and enchanted
animals that we read about in the old Slav legends: Baba Yaga
the witch, in her house on chicken's legs; the squirrel who ate
golden nuts; Tsar Saltan and his three sons; the wise cat who spoke
in verse when he turned to the left and in prose when he turned to
the right; Roussalka, the water sprite; the Golden Cockerel; these,
and many such creatures belonging to Slav legend and music.
Perhaps you know their stories through such music as Moussorgsky's
Pictures at an Exhibition, or Rimsky-Korsakov's *Tsar Saltan*, and
others. Whenever I listen to them I always imagine these legendary
characters living in the deep forests of pine and birch, under their
thick layers of snow, a world of white silence, where the creatures
all meet to enjoy snowy picnics and eat *Gogel-mogel*. A Russian
friend of mine, whose old home was in the Ukraine, near Sorot-

chinsky, the birthplace of Gogol, the immortal Russian writer (I wonder—could there be any link here—did the dish derive from the Gogol kitchens, perhaps?) told me his Nanyia used to make it this way:

4 egg yolks	$\frac{1}{4}$ teaspoon vanilla
6 tablespoons light brown sugar	(optional)

Beat the yolks of 4 eggs very, very smooth, with 6 tablespoons *light* brown sugar, and warm in a *bain marie*. That's all. Beat the mixture till it is thick, then spoon into little pots; allow to cool. If you like you can add $\frac{1}{4}$ teaspoon vanilla to the mixture when you are beating it. And I once had a Russian cook, Evgenia, who used to add some melted chocolate to the mixture, thus making it even more voluptuous, or bilious, according to the state of one's liver. In general Russian cooking is rich, complicated, and splendidly excessive, like the Slav character, and matched by their medieval architecture, the ornate gilded and coloured churches and frescoed halls. One classic early nineteenth century Russian cook-book contains a recipe which opens on this flamboyant note: *Take the yolks of five hundred eggs.* . . . I wonder what happened to the whites?

SHASHLIK (from the Caucasus)   (for 4)
  (*Wonderful for a picnic party*)

This is really just a special way of serving grilled meat—it is found all over the Near and Middle East, too, where it is called *shish kebab*. It is also a good way of making a little meat go a long way, and look very nice and different. It is especially good to do this as an outdoor dish, round the campfire, but you can also cook it under the grill of your stove. *But you must have a set of metal skewers.* You can get them at most hardware shops. The Georgian tribesmen in the Caucasus sometimes grill the meat on their swords; then throw a glass of brandy over it, and set fire to it, so that it is brought to the table

flaming. And sometimes they dance, brandishing the lighted swords, their tall black sheepskin Kolpaks cocked over on the side of their heads, as you see in my drawing—very exciting but not the sort of dance that can be done in the average kitchen.

$1\frac{1}{2}$ pounds lamb or mutton	1 onion
$\frac{1}{4}$ cup olive or salad oil	3 or 4 tomatoes
$\frac{1}{2}$ cup vinegar	Mushrooms (optional)
2 bay leaves	Bacon (optional)

The secret of a good *shashlik* is the way in which the meat is prepared overnight. Mutton or lamb is generally used, cut from the loin or shoulder. Cut $1\frac{1}{2}$ pounds into 2-inch cubes, with no fat, and let them marinate, or soak, overnight in a dish of vinegar and oil ($\frac{1}{2}$ cup vinegar, $\frac{1}{4}$ cup oil), with 2 bay leaves and an onion cut up coarsely. If possible, turn the pieces once, at least, before you leave them for the night. Next day, take them out and let them drain. The toughest meat is tender and good after this treatment.

Now thread the chunks of meat onto the skewers, and between each piece put a quarter of a tomato, or a mushroom, or even a bit of bacon, till the skewer is full. Brush the whole thing with salad oil, using a pastry brush or small clean paint-brush. The Caucasians use a little bunch of goose feathers, tied together like a tiny broom. Place your skewers on the grill (or 2 or 3 inches under the grill—high flame), turning them 2 or 3 times. They should be done in about 10 minutes. *Shashlik* is served on the skewer, usually around a big mound of plain rice. When you are ready to eat, slide the meat and tomatoes off the skewer onto your plate with a fork.

At a picnic you could substitute baked potatoes for rice (start them $\frac{1}{2}$ hour before the *shashlik*). Though they are not the traditional accompaniment, still, you will find in cooking, as in other things, that it is often necessary to find a second best, so be sure it is the best possible second best. In this case, potatoes.

By the way, you can cook fish on skewers, too: turbot, haddock, or any of the firm-fleshed fish. To prepare, cut the fish in chunks, and marinate the pieces for a few hours in a mixture of oil, onion juice, lemon juice, salt, pepper, and paprika (3 parts oil to 1 part lemon juice and dashes of the other ingredients). Put the pieces of fish on the skewer between bay leaves, and perhaps mushroom or tomato.

PASKA   (for 6)
(a Russian Easter dessert, delicious at any time)

In the old days, when Moscow rang with the bells of its thousand
churches and the air hummed with the sound, the Easter service was
the greatest of all. This was held on Saturday night, and everyone
went to church to hold a lighted candle as they sang and prayed.
Just before midnight the priests carried the Bible and the holy icons
(or portraits of the saints), in a procession round the outside of the
church, followed by a chanting choir, their faces lit by the candles
they carried. My first visit to Moscow, many years ago, was in the
summer and autumn: 'Golden-headed Moscow', says Pushkin,
speaking of the gilded domes and cupolas and crosses with their
trembling, shimmering chains, and I recall the sun glancing off
the gilding, flashing on the barbaric beauty of Vassili Blageni, outside
the Kremlin gates. But I had not yet seen Russia as I later came
to see it—in snow. Meanwhile, wherever I find myself at Easter, I
always try to go to the Russian Orthodox midnight service: Nice,
Copenhagen, Geneva, Istanbul, New York, even Los Angeles, have
churches where the singing, and Bortniansky's music is transport-
ingly lovely. In Paris there is the Russian church in the Rue Daru
where I have so often been to the lovely Easter service. On one

44

occasion, I remember being so carried away that I set fire to myself with the candle I was carrying, and was rescued by a dashing-looking stranger who beat out the flames, and later, taught me my Russian or Kyrillic alphabet in icing sugar letters, for he was an emigré who said he'd been head pastry-cook at the Winter Palace. Anyhow, he made the best *Paska* I have ever eaten, and I used to ask for it winter and summer, Christmas and Easter, though traditionally, it is eaten at Easter only, at the feast which celebrates the end of the Lenten fast. After the midnight church service is over, and everyone has kissed his neighbour three times, (a ritual my rescuer did not neglect) saying, 'Christ is Risen', everyone goes home to eat some traditional dish, above all, *Paska*. This is complicated and rich, for it requires a special sort of cream cheese and a lot of butter, and time, too. But since it is so specially delicious, I am giving you a kind of simplified version which I hope you will enjoy as much as I do when I make it each Easter. This is a party dish.

1 pound unsalted cream cheese
$\frac{1}{2}$ pint sour cream
1 cup icing sugar
$\frac{1}{2}$ teaspoon vanilla
$\frac{1}{2}$ teaspoon almond essence
1 cup seedless raisins
2 tablespoon granulated sugar

$\frac{1}{4}$ cup candied fruit (cherries, ginger, orange, candied peel, angelica, etc.)
Walnuts or chopped almonds (optional)
Crystallized cherries (optional)

Put 1 cup seedless raisins to soak in 1 tablespoon sugar and hot water. Take $\frac{1}{4}$ cup candied fruit and cut up into tiny chips, or buy the ready-chopped, mixed kind. There should be a bit of every-thing, cherries, ginger, orange, candied peel, angelica, etc. Take 1 pound cream cheese, absolutely unsalted and very fresh. Put it in a big bowl and beat it with $\frac{1}{2}$ pint sour cream. Work this very smooth and while stirring it add 1 cup icing sugar, $\frac{1}{2}$ teaspoon vanilla, and $\frac{1}{2}$ teaspoon almond essence. When the raisins seem nicely puffed up ($\frac{1}{2}$ hour or so) drain them carefully and mix into the cream, then add the chopped crystallized fruits. Mix again thoroughly. The mixture should be very firm. If it looks too creamy, add more cheese and more sugar. Pile it all up in a big, rough pyramid, forking it into shape. Leave in the refrigerator overnight, if possible. Garnish with walnuts, or blanched almonds, and whole crystallized cherries, dotted about all over the snowy mound. Traditionally, *Koulibiak* accompanies the *Paska*—it is a sort of plain, yet spicy bun-cake.

ANJOVISLÄDA (from Sweden)   (for 6)

In this northern land the long snowbound winters have only a few hours of daylight, while the short summers have no night. That is, the sun sets very late, around 11 p.m., and a pale grey-blue twilight lasts for some hours. It is never really dark, you can usually see to read all night. Then, suddenly, up comes the sun again. In the winter, there are the northern lights—the aurora borealis—flashing and glittering across the sky all night, mysterious and beautiful. This part of the world is, to me, forever peopled with the characters from Selma Lägerlöf's novels, and I always imagine a procession of sleighs racing across the snows, the terrified horses snorting and plunging, as a pack of wolves gains on them, and a beautiful creature, who bears a strong resemblance to Greta Garbo, is at last persuaded by her lover to throw out her sable muff, thus causing the wolves to lose a precious moment or two as they savage it, jewelled muff-chain and all.

In fact, however, this region is Lapland; its inhabitants are mostly reindeer herdsmen and trappers. They too drive across the ice in sleighs, but are generally pulled by reindeer (like Santa Claus) and meet the wolves with a much more practical challenge than sable muffs. They hunt them with trained eagles, great ferocious birds that perch on their shoulders, and are loosed to swoop down on the wolves to kill them in a terrible battle.

The Laps mostly eat dried meat, reindeer meat, or smoked bacon. They seldom get fresh fruit or vegetables in such a climate, except at midsummer, when there are berries growing in the forests. Once or twice a year they head south to the nearest Swedish town, where they trade their pelts, and buy groceries and provisions to last them for many months to come. They eat and drink and celebrate their visit at the inn, and this is the sort of menu they enjoy. A thick fruit soup, common to all the Baltic and Scandinavian peoples; all kinds of delicious salted fish, pickled cucumbers, specially prepared hors d'oeuvres, little tarts of ham, bits of this and that, which the Swedes love to eat before their meal (although it is really a meal in itself), called *smörgasbord*; and then, perhaps, a bacon dish followed by *anjovisläda*, an anchovy and potato pie. Here is how to make it:

47

6 large potatoes	$\frac{1}{4}$ pound butter
1 cup breadcrumbs	$\frac{1}{2}$ cup tomato purée
1 tin flat anchovies	

This is quickly and easily prepared, especially if you have some ready-cooked potatoes you want to finish up. If not, boil about 6 large ones for 20 minutes. Butter a casserole well, and sprinkle it with breadcrumbs. Cut the boiled potatoes into slices, not too thin, and arrange a layer in the casserole. Put 3 or 4 thin anchovies (tinned), some breadcrumbs, some dabs of butter, and a few teaspoons of tomato purée over the potatoes. Then put in another layer of sliced potatoes, and more anchovies, until the casserole is full. Finish with a last coating of breadcrumbs and plenty of dabs of butter all over it. Put a piece of aluminium foil or greaseproof paper over the top—this keeps it from drying too much—and cook in a medium oven for about $\frac{1}{2}$ hour.

THE HUNTER'S DISH (from Norway)   (for 2)

Perhaps this way of cooking potatoes—of making them a meal in themselves—comes from some unlucky Norwegian hunter who had spent long cold days and nights hunting for ptarmigan, or deer, or wild duck that never appeared, so that he came home hungry and disappointed to a larder empty except for potatoes. Whether he cooked the potatoes this way himself, or whether it was his wife who had been waiting patiently, hopefully, for his return, I do not know: but this is the way to do them, and very good they are. They are quite like our potato pancakes, and might serve on those occasions when everything seems to have been tried, and nothing tempts. I remember my mother used to fix the cook with a quelling glance and say: 'You had better invent a new animal today', a remark that used to fill my infant heart with the most joyous anticipation.

4 to 6 medium potatoes   2 egg yolks
1 tablespoon butter   Flour
Salt and pepper   Butter for sauté
3 tablespoons milk or cream

Take 4–6 medium-sized cooked potatoes (otherwise, boil them in salted water to cover for 20 minutes or till soft). Mash them well, with a big piece of butter, about 1 tablespoon, some salt and pepper, and 3 tablespoons milk or cream, till they are very smooth. Add 2 tablespoons of flour, and the yolks of 2 eggs. Beat all well. Drop the mixture (in large dollops first lightly floured outside) into smoking hot lard or bacon fat. Brown on both sides. I like this as a main dish: begin with a little soup, perhaps, and end with something sharp, like pineapple slices.

WINTER FRUIT SALAD (from Denmark)   (for 4)

The dish comes from a country where the summers are short and the winters long and gloomy. But this is not reflected in the charming capital, with its air of snugness and quiet gaiety; with its tiny eighteenth-century palace, guarded by bear-skinned soldiers in toy, scarlet sentry boxes; its bright-painted houses along the canals; yellow, blue, and emerald façades to corn-chandlers' shops, Chinese restaurants, tatooists' establishments, and the like; a jolly, rowdy sailors' quarter, close beside the elegant little centre, where a florid opera house is flanked by gay cafés, and old churches whose green copper spires are formed of twisted dragons, or circling stairways. No exotic fruits or vegetables grow in Denmark, though the variety of sea-food compensates. Imported dried fruits, prunes, apricots, and such, are found in all the dark little old-fashioned grocers' shops along the cobbled wharves, where there are many fish markets and sea-gulls wheel and cry and dip to snatch at the great slippery mounds of shining fish. Porridge, bread and milk, fruit soup, butter and cheese; these are everyday fare, for Denmark is a rich farming country. Bacon, too, is an everyday dish. In the long winters the children

sometimes eat hot fruit salad. It is the sort of dish I imagine one of
Hans Andersen's children enjoying; little Klaus, perhaps, as he sat
beside the big white porcelain stove that purred and roared cosily,
and outside the narrow streets were white with snow, while the poor
little match-girl longed for something as good to eat. It is very simple
to make.

1 cup dried prunes	1 cup fresh orange juice
1 cup dried apricots	3 tablespoons honey
4 medium-ripe bananas	Lemon peel
Raisins	Butter

Take 1 cup dried prunes, another of dried apricots, and put in warm water and soak for 1 hour or longer. On a big flat ovenproof dish arrange 4 medium-ripe bananas, cut in quarters. Between them put the soaked apricots and prunes and a sprinkle of raisins. Pour over the dish 1 cup fresh orange juice with 3 tablespoons honey melted and stirred in. Grate a little lemon peel and sprinkle this over everything and put some tiny dabs of butter—each the size of a small lump of sugar, about 6 of them—here and there over the fruit. Put in a moderate oven for ½ hour. Serve with or without cream.

KALLALAATIKO (from Finland)   (for 4)

In Finland, the long icy winters are such that everybody's first thought is how to keep warm. A lot of pork is eaten, for there is an old saying: 'Pork keeps you warm, and warmth keeps you loving'. The Finns also keep warm by means of special steam baths called *Saunas*, which people today add to their gardens much as Americans do swimming pools. The *Saunas* are a fearfully hot steamy business (rather like Turkish baths), but after an hour or so some Finns have the courage to rush out quite naked and roll themselves in the snow. This is said to be splendid for the circulation, but I would rather not try it myself. I have a Finnish friend who lives on Long Island (New York), and she has built herself a *Sauna* bath on the back porch. I asked her if she rolled naked in the snow, and what the neighbours thought of it all, but she side-tracked me by saying there had not been any snow since her *Suana* was built. She keeps many of her Finnish ways and often cooks Finnish food. *Kallalaatiko* is one of her favourite dishes.

4 pork chops	2 eggs
2 fresh herrings	2 cups milk
4 medium potatoes	1 tablespoon flour
4 onions	Pinch of salt and pepper
Butter	

Take 4 pork chops and 2 fresh herrings. Split the herrings and remove the backbone; cut off heads and tails (of course you can get the fishmonger to do this for you). Now peel and slice 4 medium-sized potatoes rather thin. Do the same with 4 onions. Butter a casserole, place in it a layer of potatoes and one of onion. Lay in 2 pork chops, then 2 halves of herring, then another layer of potato and onion. For the next layer put in your other 2 pork chops with the remaining 2 halves of herring. Fill in around and cover the top with the remains of the onion and potato. Dot with a little butter. Put in a medium hot oven for 1 hour, uncovered. Then beat 2 eggs with 2 cups milk; add 1 tablespoon flour (be sure the flour is worked in absolutely smoothly with no lumps left), add a pich of salt and pepper, and pour over the casserole so that it sinks right through and makes a layer on top. Put the casserole back in a medium hot oven for about ½ hour, until the custard is firm. Then your *kallalaatiko* is done.

LITTLE PIGS OF HEAVEN (from Spain*) (for 4)

This is a heavenly sweet, not easy to make, but well worth it. I wish I knew how it got its name, but I don't; perhaps because the little sweets look fat, piglike, and are so delicious to eat. It is alleged to come from Andalusia, which Stendhal said was one of the haunts that pleasure has marked for its own on earth. When the Moors abandoned Andalusia they left behind a strong Arab flavour, in music, architecture, and food: the strange harsh cries and monotonous quarter-tones of Spanish singing, the houses built round tiled patios and fountain courts, and the excessively sweet dishes—all these show a Moorish origin. Make the Little Pigs this way.

½ cup sugar	2 small bars chocolate
1 cup warm water	1 cup boiling water
6 egg yolks	1 teaspoon vanilla

* By courtesy of Countess Morphy.

53

Put ½ cup sugar and 1 cup warm water in a saucepan and boil fast until a sort of thick syrup is formed; when you can lift the spoon and pull up a long, fine thread of this syrup, almost as if it were a piece of delicate string, the syrup is ready. Take it off the fire and set aside to cool. Beat the yolks of 6 eggs. When the syrup is cool add eggs slowly to it, stirring constantly (if it is too hot, you will spoil your dish). Put this mixture into little fireproof dishes—cocottes —glass or earthenware. Stand these in a big saucepan or even a big deep frying pan. Fill the saucepan with water halfway up the sides of the little dishes. Be very careful about this, or when the water starts to boil it will bubble up and get into your pigs. Do not cover the pan.

Keep the water boiling, but not too furiously. When the mixture seems firm (test it with a knife), remove the little dishes. Wear a cooking glove to do this, or use tongs. Leave them to cool off. Then turn the piglets out (by running a warmed knife round their edges and turn them upside down on a platter). Pour warm chocolate sauce over them. For this, either use a ready-made one or make it by dissolving plain eating chocolate in a cup of boiling water and add a teaspoon of vanilla extract, but no sugar. Heat this slowly, stirring all the time. (Or you could use a good jam, heated.) When hot, *but not boiling*, pour over the Little Pigs of Heaven . . . heavenly, indeed, and sweet enough for any turbanned Moor.

CARMEN'S CHESTNUT SOUP (from Spain)   (for 4)

That is how it is named in one of my oldest, most tattered cook-books, written a hundred years or so before Prosper Merimée described his immortal character of that name: though there could be no con-nection, I feel, between Merimée's Carmen and any recipe. She was not the domestic type. Unfortunately, she has become diluted by a series of orchestral extracts and we forget both her dynamism and Bizet's original force. Whenever I hear the strains of *L'amour est l'enfant de bohème* rising above the clatter of coffee-cups in palmy courts, I remember her violent behaviour, her amoral nature, forgotten by most casual listeners who have come to accept her as some vaguely Spanish symbol—the apotheosis of Fancy Dress, swirling skirts, and towering comb, biting up a carnation.

I don't suppose Carmen ever cooked anything. The only occasion Merimée describes her indoors (except in the cigarette factory, where she and her knife caused such havoc) is that scalding passage with the spellbound Don José, when, gathering up a sort of picnic of bon-bons, cakes, and wines, she leads him off to a bare room in a squalid street in old Seville. There, between kisses, she flings the dishes at the ceiling to kill the flies, and gathering up the broken pieces, uses them as castanets to accompany a wild cachucha. No, emphatically not the domestic type. Still, had she cooked anything, I think this chestnut soup might have been in character.

4 pounds chestnuts	Salt, and black pepper
A chunk of bacon	A pinch of mace
½ pound of veal for stewing	1 teaspoon brown sugar
1 onion	10 cups of veal or beef stock
1 carrot	(or the equivalent in a good tinned broth)

Roast your chestnuts over a slow fire, or in the oven, around ½ hour—they must not burn. Peel them, and put them to stew gently in the stock. In another stew-pan, put the chunk of bacon, the veal, cut in small squares, the carrot, onion, herbs, mace, pepper, and salt, and let it cook until it begins to stick to the pan; the bacon fat will melt enough to prevent it burning, for a while. Then add 3 cups of broth and cook all together fast, uncovered, so that it reduces a little. In about ½ hour add it to the chestnuts, now tender, in their broth. Let the whole thing simmer, covered, for another 15 minutes: add a small teaspoon of sugar just before serving. According to another eighteenth century cook-book 'A good Spanish cook will shred a pheasant and a brace of partridges to enrich it somewhat'. Few of us will be such good cooks as that, I feel. Let us content ourselves with the more modest version. Don't forget, when serving, to strain your soup, removing meat and vegetables—but replace some of the chestnuts, to garnish.

FISHERMAN'S LEMONS (from Portugal)   (for 4)

All along the coast of Portugal enormous Atlantic breakers pound in onto sandy beaches or pink rock coves where fishermen mend their nets, and set out to sea in curiously curved boats, often adorned with a large painted eye, to help the boat find fish, it is held. Oporto (from which port wine gets its name) is full of animation, with ships loading barrels of this nourishing brew, and Lisbon has beautiful yellow and blue tiled houses and a magnificent carriage museum filled with elaborate gold state coaches, landaus, open carriages, shut carriages, and every kind of sedan. But I prefer the Portuguese villages, little whitewashed houses, often dominated by a windmill, and surrounded by cork woods.

One fishing village such as these, in the extreme south, used to hold a sort of midnight fish-feast, or sardine-saturnalia if the catch had been particularly good. Tunny and sardine were the most rewarding haul. A look-out man wearing a red-tasselled cap would

shout to the village when the fishing fleet's lights were sighted, coming in. The whole population would rush down to the beach to meet them and help drag in the boats. The fish would be auctioned off, there and then, by the light of torches or lamps. Buyers from the city, or foreign markets bid against each other in an atmosphere of tension and hostility. No sooner bought than packed and piled on carts, the fish was rushed off to the nearest railway station (some eleven miles away) where the night express paused just long enough to pick up the fishy loads. Meanwhile, on the beach, a splendid saturnalia was in full swing. Everyone gathered round a huge bon-fire, to roast (on little sticks) the remains of the sardine catch. The innkeeper dispensed wine and an old woman produced a vast basket full of bread. As we ate, some one else produced a guitar, and they all began to sing their traditional *fados*, those beautiful songs that recall the softer sort of Gypsy music, with an almost Oriental or Turkish cadence of melancholy. The fresh sardines we ate, then, had little to do with the tinned kind; but I never, now, see a box of sardines without recalling those all-night feasts on that Portuguese beach.

Portuguese cooking is somewhat similar to Spanish; oranges and lemons and walnuts are cheap: fish is a staple. Fish soups, and the more solid cod, or tuna, are generally eaten with rice. One of their simple, but delicious ways of beginning a meal comes from a small hotel at Cintra, near Lisbon. Cintra is considered so beautiful that an old proverb says: 'To see the world and not see Cintra, is to travel blindfolded'.

4 big lemons	1 teaspoon lemon juice
¾ cup cooked or tinned fish	1 egg, hard-boiled
2 tablespoons mayonnaise	Radishes or watercress

Take 4 big lemons, cut them in half, squeeze out the juice, and scoop out all the pulp. Take ¾ cup tinned salmon or leftover cooked fish; be sure it has no bones in it, and mix it with 2 tablespoons mayonnaise and 1 teaspoon lemon juice. Fill the lemon halves with the mixture, and sprinkle chopped hard boiled egg on top. If you use sardines for the filling, don't use mayonnaise—it will be too rich.

To serve the stuffed lemons, cut the rounded bottom off, so they stand firm like eggcups. Surround them with radishes or green salad leaves. Watercress is even better than lettuce. Eat with brown bread and butter.

And here is another first course from Cintra:

PORTUGUESE EGGS (for 4)

4 large tomatoes	Butter
4 eggs	Salt and pepper
¼ cup breadcrumbs	Parsley

Choose very large, firm tomatoes, cut off the tops, scoop out the centre, and carefully break an egg into each. Try not to break the yolk. Add salt and pepper, sprinkle with breadcrumbs and chopped parsley and dab with butter. Arrange on a greased fireproof dish and bake in a medium oven for about 15 minutes—till eggs are well set. It is important that the tomatoes are ripe ones, or they will be hard and seem uncooked. On the other hand, if you use over-ripe ones, they will burst, so aim at a happy medium. Serve with a cheese sauce (see p. 169).

RISOTTO (from Italy) (for 4)

The rice for risotto should be round, Aboria, while for a pilaff, a Patna or long-grain rice is best (see p. 89). These two ways of cooking rice are entirely different. The pilaff is a *dry*, fluffy rice; the risotto is creamy, almost sticky, and soft. This is the great Italian speciality, along with spaghetti or macaroni.

Risotto can be made with little pieces of ham, or chicken livers, or mushrooms, or just grated cheese. The cheese one I like best I used to eat in the north of Italy, in Bologna, always famous for its wonderful cooking, and where there are all kinds of delicious sausages.

Bologna, '*dark, many-towered Bologna*', as Carducci called it, is bitterly cold in winter, and many of the streets are arcaded to protect passers-by as much from the snow and rain and cold winds as from the hot summer sun. Bologna, too, is famous for being the home of the first troupes of mummers, dancers, and singers, players who became known to all the world as Harlequin and Columbine, Clown and Pantaloon. Imagine them, this poor but gay little band, washing

59

off their greasepaint after a show, and getting out of their spangles and masks and gaudy clothes, to hurry along under the dark, draughty arcaded streets to some little *trattoria*, or inn, where they all have supper together and perhaps practise a new song, to the accompaniment of a guitar—pretty much as today you might see a touring theatrical company eating their belated supper at a snack-bar, each earnestly discussing the merits of their own performance. These Italian players, and any of the famous eighteenth-century company known as the *Commedia del'Arte*, would probably have eaten risotto, and drunk a cheap red wine. This is how to cook a *Risotto Parmesan*—that is, with parmesan cheese.

1 large onion	Butter
2 tablespoons butter	Parmesan cheese, grated
1¼ cups Aboria rice	Cooked ham or mushrooms
1 teaspoon saffron powder	(optional)
2½ cups clear chicken broth or consommé	

Sauté a large chopped onion in 1 tablespoon butter and add to it 1¼ cups Aboria rice. (Don't wash the rice.) Turn the heat very low and add another tablespoon of butter. When the rice has soaked up all the fat, add ½ teaspoon saffron powder. This will turn the rice a bright yellow and add a very delicate flavour. Add 1 cup clear chicken broth or consommé, the packet, or tinned kind will do beautifully, though any clear meat broth is all right. Cover the pan and cook the rice very, very slowly (asbestos mat) until all the liquid has been absorbed. Then add ½ cup more; when this is gone, add another ½ cup, so that, in all, you have used about 2½ cups of stock to 1¼ cups of rice. Stir it with a wooden spoon each time you add liquid, but stir carefully—don't mash it. When there is no more liquid left, your risotto is ready to eat. Turn it out into a bowl and dot it with butter, and add plenty of grated parmesan cheese; if you can, stir in some bits of lean cooked ham, or some mushrooms sautéed for 10 minutes and cut in quarters.

FISH SAUCE FOR SPAGHETTI (from Naples)   (for 4)

Everyone will tell you that the simplest dish to make is spaghetti.
You have only to follow the directions on the package. To make a
sauce out of tomato purée is simple, too, and meat sauce for spaghetti,
also, is not difficult. But did you know the Italians sometimes make
a fish sauce to eat with their spaghetti? This is how they do it in
Naples, in the tall pink and yellow houses all around the harbour,
where rags of washing always hang across the narrow chasm streets
like flags, and the overcrowded rooms have a film of fine ash all over
them when the wind blows from across the bay where Vesuvius
smokes and puffs and rumbles and sometimes bursts into flames.
No one thinks about the awful damage it may do if one day it erupts
again; so they go on living their usual way, laughing, quarrelling,
and singing. The Neapolitans sing, dance, and play the guitar on
all occasions and still perform traditional dances such as the taran-
tella—though American swing has now become far more popular.
Here is their fish sauce.

½ cup salad oil

1 large clove garlic

1 tablespoon butter

1 tin anchovies

Yolks of 3 hard-boiled eggs

Pinch of pepper

½ cup chopped parsley

Juice of ½ lemon

Take ½ cup salad oil (for this you could use olive oil), crush a whole large clove of garlic in it, add 1 tablespoon butter and heat all together over a low flame for 2 or 3 minutes. Add a small tin of anchovies and their oil. Mash them into the oil with a wooden spoon; when they are well mashed, add the yolks of 3 hard-boiled eggs and mash them in, too. Add plenty of black pepper and ½ cup chopped fresh parsley. Cook together for another minute, and when you take them off the flame, add the juice of ½ a small lemon. Serve hot, of course, with your spaghetti, noodles, or macaroni.

FRANGIPANI (from Sicily) (for 4)

Sicily is mostly a very bare rocky place with volcanic peaks and some orange groves. Sicilians live by fishing and a bit of farming, and have few amusements. Perhaps there are now numbers of cinemas, but when I was there, there was nothing of the kind. The people like to decorate their carts with bright-painted scenes, mermaids and monsters, flowers and fruits. There is one great excitement—the puppet theatre—the Teatro dei Piccoli. This has been going on for centuries, the same characters, the same stories. The same families carry on the business, and each generation learns the art of working the puppets and imitating the different voices, singing basso for the villain, and soprano for the heroine. The puppets are very large ones, often almost as big as a live person, and wear wonderful costumes, golden armour for the knights, jewelled crowns and velvet robes for the princesses. They endure terrible adventures before the happy ending, when the audience troops out into the ill-lit, whitewashed streets and goes home to bed. On the way home, they often stop at a *trattoria*, and eat a specially heavy sort of chestnut cake and drink a glass of red wine or a cup of coffee as a nightcap.

After one show I was invited to eat with the owner of the puppets, Papa Guiseppi. I felt greatly honoured. We sat behind the scenes, among the marionettes and their tangled strings and dusty velvet garments. Papa Guiseppi was mending a tin sword, bent in the violence of a battle. His daughter, Tommasina, was heating some curling irons, to crimp the long golden wig worn by the Queen. As they worked they sang songs from the Sicilian opera *Cavalleria Rusticana*. It is about the Sicilian peasants, and is known and loved all over the world, not just in Sicily. Alessandro, another member of the family, offered me a glass of wine and an exotic sweet cut in little squares, which he called *frangipani*, at which an old, old lady, his great-grandmother, who was asleep in a corner, suddenly woke up and said she had made it herself. This is how she did it.

3 eggs	5 tablespoons icing sugar
3 tablespoons flour	5 tablespoons ground
2 cups milk	almonds

Beat 3 eggs together, add 3 tablespoons flour, mixed in a little cold milk, and stir carefully into the eggs. Add 2 cups milk, and heat in the double boiler, stirring all the time. Cook it slowly for 15 minutes. During this time add, bit by bit, 5 tablespoons fine powdered sugar and the same amount of ground almonds. When the whole thing is a thick, smooth mixture, remove and pour it into a flat baking dish. Let it get quite cold, and then cut into small squares, like Turkish Delight.

SARDINIAN SPINACH   (for 4)

My outstanding memory of Sardinia is the local breed of donkeys, very small, the size of large dogs; cream-coloured creatures that trot about the lanes pulling small carts full of firewood, or fish, or vegetables, or any other domestic commodity. Their ears are enormous and furry, their hooves the smallest, neatest ones imaginable. In wet weather Sardinia is as disagreeable as all the other Mediterranean countries, which belong basically to the sunshine and are in no way equipped for cold or wet (both of which occur with dismal regularity in winter). Blanketing white sea-mists conceal the lovely views across the Gulf of Cagliari, removing all the colour, while raging winds seep under the ill-fitting doors, turning into draughts as they approach human habitation. The olive groves drip softly in the rain: mud deepens rapidly. Fires smoke; the village store runs short of candles. There is nothing—absolutely nothing—to do but eat and sleep, and wait for the sun. Suddenly it flashes forth once more, radiant, revitalizing, reassuring, and we forget past discomforts. We climb the hills to a pink-washed village and order lunch. There is not much left, says the proprietor: the butcher has not been up for a week: the fishing has been poor: goats' cheese— wine—an omelette? Yes, that will do nicely. We sit on the terrace under a yellowing vine and soak up the sun. Presently he brings us food, and as an extra dish, spinach and rice—leftovers, he says, apologizing, quite unnecessarily, for it is delicious.

3 cups cooked spinach, chopped fine
1 cup cooked rice
Salt and pepper to taste
2 eggs
2 or 3 tablespoons grated cheese
2 tablespoons melted butter
Flour
4–6 tablespoons oil

Chop 3 cups cooked spinach very fine. Mix with 1 cup cooked rice. Add salt and pepper. Add 2 eggs, well beaten, 2 or 3 tablespoons grated cheese, 2 tablespoons melted butter. Mix well and shape into little round flat cakes (croquettes, as they are called). Flour them lightly and sauté them in about 4–6 tablespoons oil, 2 or 3 minutes on each side, until they are a light golden colour. Turn them carefully, with a spatula. Serve them, perhaps, with a salad of endive, and thin rounds of orange, with sugar, oil, and lemon dressing (see p. 6).

THE BALKANS

IMAM BÄILDI (from Turkey)   (for 6)

There is an odd idea in the West that Eastern and Near Eastern
cooking is unhealthy. This is quite wrong. Except for certain very
sugary sweets, it is not even rich. Grilled meat, rice, vegetables,
yoghourt—this is the basis of Turkish cooking. Two principal dishes
are *dolma* (stuffed vegetables), and *shish kebab* (meat grilled on a
shish, or skewer). Variations of these are found all over the Near
and Middle East, from the Caucasus in southern Russia to Egypt.
Don't forget that Turkish cooking is considered one of the basic
cuisines of the world, with French, Chinese, and Italian. From these
all the rest are said to derive. And don't forget, too, that it was the
Turks who, when they took Vienna by siege, first introduced the
cafés, or restaurants where coffee was drunk, and for which in later
centuries Vienna became so celebrated.

Perhaps the most popular of all Turkish dishes (beside their coffee
and the widely known and exported Eastern sweet, *Rahout Lokoum*,
or Turkish Delight) is *Imam bäildi*, which means the imam, or priest,
swooned. Why? Because the dish prepared for him by his proud host
was so exquisite, so perfect, that the worthy gentleman was overcome. But we are not told whether he fainted before or after eating
the dish, from excitement or from overeating. In general, I have
found Turkish appetites robust. In the little restaurants overlooking
the Marmora, in a quarter of Istanbul little visited by tourists,
the fishermen sit eating heartily and watching, with fixed, trancy
eyes, the undulations of a series of very roundabout ladies, whose
belly-dances are accompanied by an Asiatic orchestra. The hors
d'oeuvres alone cram the table with dishes of every imaginable
delicacy, and is a meal in itself. Last time I was in Istanbul I used
to cross the Bosphorus very early in the summer sunrise, to breakfast
with a friend whose *yali* or summer villa overhung the water at
Beylerbey. Here, in a little Turkish rococo kiosque, I used to find
the sort of gargantuan breakfast I have seen Leicestershire house-
parties demolish before the hunt; but which made me feel as faint
as the Imam. The splendid, climbing sun would gild at least three
kinds of meat: fish, eggs, cheese, a number of cakes and pastries,

fruit, and the ritual glasses of tea, filled and refilled from the purring samovar.

Below, the water slapped at the steps of the landing stage, and the big blue-painted caiques began to leave their moorings and head upstream towards the Black Sea, for a day's fishing, the crew singing as they went. We used to watch them till they were lost to sight beyond the Sweet Waters of Asia. . . . Breakfast in Asia! it sounds exotic—it was exotic: but it used to take all day to recover from such a start.

As to the fatal dish which prostrated the imam, in plain language it is stuffed aubergine (you could substitute vegetable marrow).

3 medium aubergines
(eggplants)
Salt and pepper to taste
½ cup olive oil
4 large onions
¾ cup water
6 teaspoons tomato purée
½ cup breadcrumbs
½ teaspoon salt
Pinch of pepper
½ teaspoon curry powder
2 tablespoons olive oil
1 tablespoon pine kernels
or chopped almonds or
peanuts
Chopped parsley
Black olives, stoned

Choose medium-sized eggplants: 3 for 6 people. Plunge them into boiling water, to cover, and cook for 15 minutes. Take them out, plunge them into cold water for 3 minutes. Then cut them lengthwise. With a spoon, scoop out all the centre, leaving only a shell about ½ inch thick, of outside skin and pulp. Put them in a casserole dish, add salt and pepper, and pour ½ cup olive oil over them. Then cook in a medium oven for about 30 minutes. During this time prepare the stuffing.

For this, chop up the insides you took out of the eggplant shells. Take 4 big onions, cut up finely, and cook them in a very little water, about ¾ of a cup. When they are soft (8–10 minutes), add 6 teaspoons tomato purée (or fresh tomatoes cooked in water, like the onions), ½ cup breadcrumbs, the mashed eggplant pulp, and mix together. Add ½ teaspoon salt, a pinch of pepper, ½ teaspoon curry powder, and 2 tablespoons olive oil (and 1 tablespoon pine kernels if you can get them). Stir well, and put in a frying pan and cook gently for about 20 minutes. Then take the eggplant shells out of the oven carefully: they should be firm and look rather like little boats. Fill them with the mixture, pour over them any oil left in the pan in which they were cooked; sprinkle with a little chopped parsley, and, if you like, add a few stoned black olives. Let them cool slowly: *but not in the refrigerator.* They are best eaten some hours later when they have settled, though they can be eaten hot, as soon as cooked.

I expect the imam finished off his meal with a little cup of Turkish coffee, some dried figs from Smyrna, a piece of Turkish Delight, and perhaps some *baklava*, a sweet with nuts and honey. And I dare say he also had some of those little pastries known as Beauty's Lips, which are shaped like a mouth and fried in oil and rolled in syrup. After which I am not surprised to learn he swooned.

ROSE-LEAF JAM

This exquisite treat is made and enjoyed all over the Near East and in the Balkans. A few enterprising grocers stock it, but it is generally difficult to find, so I shall give you an old recipe given me in Turkey, where roses are grown not only for perfume but for jam, too. The jam is best eaten as an accompaniment to yoghourt—very little, for it is exceedingly sweet. Indeed, its use as a traditional offering to guests on arrival is said to derive from the fact that its excessive sweetness produces a thirst: this, it is inferred, will be slaked by the host's best wine.

3 cups rose petals	1 tablespoon lemon juice
3 cups white sugar	1 cup rose-water

Choose the finest red or pink roses. Be sure that the petals are free of insects. Cram them down tight into the cup when you measure. Now take 3 cups sugar, 1 cup rose-water (from the chemist), and the lemon juice, and mix in a big bowl. When the sugar has dissolved, mix in the rose petals, and stand this 'in the rays of the midday sun,' as I was told. Otherwise, at the back of the stove, not over direct flame, till it has all dissolved together into a gooey jam. Now put it in a saucepan and cook over a very low flame for ½ hour, stirring all the time, for it burns easily. When the petals are transparent, or melted, put to cool, and then turn into little glass jars and cover. If you keep these in the refrigerator, take them out an hour or so before serving, so that they warm to room temperature.

POOR MAN'S CAVIAR (from Roumania)   (for 4)

The Danube, as one of the great rivers of Europe, runs through, several different countries on its way to the Black Sea. As it flows through Vienna they call it the Blue Danube, though it always looks like a muddy grey to me. When it reaches 'The Iron Gates,' a narrow rock defile which guards the entrance to Roumania, the Danube becomes a deep green; but as it widens out to the delta country, becoming a mighty, slow-moving waterway recalling the Missis- sippi, it becomes a thick yellowish expanse, bordered by sandbanks and endless steppes, or prairies, where there is no sign of man. At Valçov, on the Black Sea, which really is a dark inky colour, though named Black for its treacherous nature as much as its hue, it merges into salt lagoons, like tropic mangrove-swamp country, where the fishermen live by preparing caviar, that very rare expensive delicacy that is exported all over the world but which only the rich can afford to buy. Caviar is supposed to be a Russian specialty, the finest coming from Beluga, on the Caspian Sea. I have one Russian friend who left the country very young, during the Revolution, in a great hurry, leaving all her belongings behind. But she managed to snatch up her favourite little gold caviar spoon, and to keep it for years. It was only during a particularly bad spell that she was at last compelled to sell it. Now fortunately in a position to buy caviar from time to time, she tells me that somehow it never tastes the same since it is no longer eaten with a golden spoon.

I too, have had some opportunities to eat caviar in an exceptional way—in bulk, that is. When we were *en poste* in Sofia, immediately after the war, the Russian generals used to give splendid parties where they served wash-bowls full of caviar—the best Beluga. I had the sensation of plunging headlong into such richness. Vodka flowed, and afterwards there was dancing, that exuberant rubber-bouncing of the Cossacks: gopaks, and all kinds of stamping, savage, and joyous rhythms that are in the Russian blood. I remember trying to teach some Cossack officers *Sir Roger de Coverley*, from which they made their own sort of *furiante* ; excellent for shaking off the effects of over-eating.

The kind of caviar that comes from Valçov is very good indeed, and almost as *recherché*. Although the fishermen have to work hard to catch the huge sturgeon whose eggs are in fact what we know as caviar, they are much too poor to eat any of it themselves. The eggs are cut out of the fish, roughly washed in the stream, salted, packed in tins, put on ice (no refrigerators there), and rushed to the train. In summer the heat in this part of Roumania, known as the Dobrudja, is fierce. Yet in winter there are sometimes snow-storms, and wolves howling round. I know, for I have seen and heard both.

In summer, when their day's work is done, the Valçov fishermen and their families settle down outside their wooden huts, where huge sunflowers line the white fences that surround the little gardens, and streams or canals flow past the gates, for there are more waterways than roads here. They eat their simple supper by the light of a lantern, and in the dark you hear them singing their wild, wonderful songs, part Gypsy, which if you have once heard you can never forget, and which torment you for the rest of your days.

Roumanian food is excellent and has many special dishes, such as crayfish cooked in saffron; *mitite*, a sausage dish; and *mamaliglia* (a sort of doughy, cakey mush). But the majority of the people eat very simply: black bread, garlic, vegetables, gigantic watermelons that grow everywhere in the Balkans, and a glass of tea from a samovar, in the Russian manner. One of their typical foods is made from aubergine, and known as Poor Man's Caviar. This is about as near to eating the real thing as they can get. Anyway, it is delicious. Make it this way.

2 large aubergines	½ teaspoon salt
4 tablespoons oil	Pepper and paprika
2 tablespoons lemon juice (or vinegar)	1 large onion, chopped

Take 2 big aubergines. Put them in the oven, rather a hot one, until they are soft. The time depends on how big they are, around 45 minutes *at least*. (You can also boil them in water, but I prefer them roasted in the oven.) Now peel them, mash up the inside, forking it round and round till it is absolutely smooth, with 4 tablespoons oil, 2 tablespoons lemon juice or vinegar, ½ teaspoon salt, a shake of pepper and paprika.

When all this is absolutely smooth, cut up *very thin* and chop into tiny bits 1 large raw onion and stir this into the mixture, which must be allowed to get really cold. Then the Poor Man's Caviar is ready—and good enough for the richest man to enjoy. Eat it as a salad, with black or brown bread and butter, and maybe plain watercress or sliced tomato. With this, mayonnaise would be redundant.

I think a lovely meal for a summer night would be jellied consommé, Poor Man's Caviar and black bread and butter, and some cheese. To finish, watermelon, sprinkled with powdered sugar and ginger. You might serve Turkish coffee to round off the menu.

STUFFED ONIONS (from Bucharest)   (for 4)

Here is a kidney and onion dish as I ate it in Bucharest at a little, bright-lit, noisy restaurant beside the markets where no booth ever seemed to shut (nor did the city ever seem to sleep, for that matter), and where the Gypsies strutted about, beautiful and diabolic, playing their violins savagely, and making, with equal savagery, their poor performing bears hop and lumber for pennies. More Gypsies squatted along the kerb selling huge bunches of flowers, and rugs—the celebrated Bessarabian Aubusson which are just as bright and bunched with flowers as the Gypsies' baskets. I have longed for such rugs all my life—but there, confronted at last by them, we were also confronted by problems of inflation, exchange, devaluation. . . . At that moment, no one could work out how much, or little, the *lei* was worth. The Gypsies asked several million of them for a rug: but were there one, or two, or even three million *lei* to the pound sterling? Was it an astronomic price, or given away? No one was able to face such intricacies. The menu was problem enough. So I retired beaten to the restaurant kitchen, where a French-speaking cook let me watch his scullions at work—Gypsies here, too, their glittering-sharp eyes peering in from the yard, where people were plucking poultry, or gutting fish at the pump. And over all, as over all Bucharest, challenging and conquering the blasts from the ovens, hung that heady, drenching perfume, combination of expensive French scents and cheap local essences, hair oil, and the make-up which was the most striking aspect of the crowds swarming about their nocturnal business. Just as, in the Midi, an overpowering blast of garlic, digestively speaking most beneficent, and socially speaking all-pervading, strikes the newcomer as being the very essence of the land, so, in Bucharest, it was this heady perfume, exhaled by not only the more seductive female passers-by, but by trim, richly-medalled officers, coachmen, and policemen too; all of them swam in musk and patchouli and *violette de parme*. The cook, who mopped his brow with a cotton handkerchief reeking of attar of roses, gave me several recipes: this is the onion and kidney dish.

4 large onions
4 lamb kidneys, chopped
Salt and pepper
4 cloves
Nutmeg

4 pinches of mixed dried herbs
4 pats of butter
4 teaspoons olive oil
Chopped parsley

Choose very large onions—the largest you can find. Peel them and cook in boiling water to cover for at least 20 minutes. Take them out and carefully scoop out their centres leaving a shell about $\frac{1}{2}$ inch thick; stuff these with lamb kidneys (1 to each onion), chopped into very small pieces. Add salt and pepper, 1 clove, a little chopped parsley, a generous pinch of nutmeg, and a pinch of mixed dried herbs to each. Put a dab of butter on top. Now stand the onions in a greased casserole; choose a rather small one, so that they are tightly packed in. This keeps them from collapsing. Put a teaspoon of oil over each, and more salt and pepper; put a lid on the casserole and bake them in a medium oven for another $\frac{3}{4}$ hour, or until they seem really done. I suggest triangles of fried bread as an extra.

BANDIT'S JOY (Honeyed Potatoes) (from Albania)   (for 4)

I must confess that I was once rather friendly with a bandit in the Balkans, in the mountain country west of Macedonia. He had behaved so badly that he could no longer come down to the village where his family lived, for both the police and the soldiers were after him. But, as I knew his sister, she used to take me with her when she visited him in his mountain hideout, bringing him cartridges for his gun—with which, we hope, he shot only hares or game. He was a very handsome creature, and always dressed most elaborately. His head was shaved, but he had enormous black moustachios. He wore the white felt cap most Albanians wear, at least three embroidered jackets, a sash stuck with knives, tasselled trousers, and over all a huge shaggy sheepskin coat. He always carried a rifle of which he seemed very proud, and round the barrel he had hung a string of bright blue beads, such as are generally hung on the horses' harnesses in the Near East, to ward off the evil eye, it is said. His name was Salko, and he and his sister used to cry with joy when they met and then start talking about politics, always sounding very angry. Sometimes I persuaded them to tell me stories of the historic battles between the Albanians and their traditional Turkish enemies, or the feuds between one border-raiding party and another. The Balkans used to be peopled with such wild bands as the Pallikares, the Bashi-Bazouks, the Comitadjis, the Skreli, or the Miriditi, many of whom were to be found living in the Mountains of the Accursed. It all sounds very theatrical, but that part of the world is like that.

Salko's sister used sometimes to take him a dish she had prepared for him. It was his favourite food, but it seemed a very odd choice for such a violent man, being made of honey and potatoes. This is how she made it.

4 large (sweet or ordinary) potatoes	Grated nutmeg
4 tablespoons butter	$\frac{1}{2}$ cup honey
	Juice $\frac{1}{2}$ lemon

The potatoes were first parboiled, that is, quickly boiled in water for about 10 minutes. Then they were peeled and cut into thick, chunky slices. Next they were fried in butter till golden brown, then powdered with grated nutmeg, and eaten with warm honey (the Macedonian honey was a rich, dark green colour, I recall), with the juice of $\frac{1}{2}$ a lemon squeezed into it.

SOUTLIASH (from Bulgaria)   (for 4)

Perhaps the best known thing about Bulgaria is that it produces most of the world's supply of rose essence—that most lovely of perfumes, so strong, so precious, that a mere drop of it forms the base for quite a lot of other perfumes. The flowers grow in a valley known as the Rose Valley: it is about twenty miles wide and nearly a hundred miles long, and as you drive toward it from very far away an overpowering, delicious rose fragrance is carried on the wind. Then your road climbs down from the foothills of the Rhodope Mountains—and suddenly you see the pink haze of the famous Rose Valley stretching before you. In the early part of June the rose-pickers work all day, from dawn to dusk, gathering the petals in huge sacks and carting them to the distilleries in the little town of Kazanluk, where, in the shadow of the great walnut trees, the tired rose-pickers eat their supper. It is so beautiful there, that when I remember those evenings, like Zarathustra, I grow sád at sunset. A traditional Bulgarian dish is *soutliash*, which is almost what we call rice pudding. I think their way of making it is very good.

1 cup rice	1 cup sour cream
2 cups milk	1 teaspoon vanilla extract
2 tablespoons white sugar	Cherry jam (optional)

If you have any leftover cooked rice, here is a way to use it up. Otherwise, boil 1 cup rice in 2 cups milk, with 1 tablespoon white sugar. Cook for 20 minutes; drain off the milk. Let the rice get cold. Now beat it up with 1 cup sour cream, add another tablespoon of sugar and 1 teaspoon vanilla extract. When the rice is a rich, creamy mass, chill it thoroughly, and serve with or without jam. The Bulgarians I knew served little spoonfuls of rose-leaf jam with their *soutliash*, but cherry jam would be just as good.

TARATOR (from Bulgaria) (for 4)

In the Balkan countries, Yugoslavia, Roumania, Bulgaria, Albania, and Greece, one of the great specialities is yoghourt. Add bread and onions and olives, and you have the main diet of the Balkan people. Yoghourt is a sort of sour milk, rather complicated to make yourself, but to be obtained from most dairies today. It is one of the most delicious and wholesome foods in the world. Many Balkan people live to be well over a hundred and are still very strong and active: they always tell you it is because they have so much yoghourt. It can be eaten many ways, as a sauce with meat; as a dessert with jam or fruit. There are various kinds of yoghourt. The best is made with sheep's milk rather than cow's milk. The Balkan people like to eat it with a piece of bread—nothing else, so they can really taste the subtle flavour, very much as in the Near East, water, pure water, is considered a supreme treat, the subtle differences in this well or that source being discussed as if they were vintage wines. Nile water for, I think, 1821, is still regarded as a memorable brew. The Bulgarians serve yoghourt as a cold soup.

2 or 3 cucumbers	Salt and pepper to taste
1 heaping teaspoon salt	1 clove garlic
4 jars yoghourt	Chopped walnuts

Peel 2 or 3 cucumbers, slice medium thin, about $\frac{1}{4}$ inch thick (not the very thin slices used for sandwiches). Put them in a bowl, sprinkle plenty of salt over them, about 1 heaping teaspoon, to make all the water run out. Leave the bowl in the refrigerator until just before you are ready to eat. Next, take 4 jars of yoghourt (or 1 for each person), mix together in a big bowl, add salt and pepper to taste. Cut up a big clove of garlic into tiny chips and sprinkle into the yoghourt. Stir well. Now get the cucumber slices, drain off the liquid, and mix the cucumber into the yoghourt. Decorate with a few slices arranged on the top, at the last moment, to look nice and cool and green. Sprinkle with chopped walnuts, and serve at once while it is very cold.

SARMA (from Yugoslavia)   (for 6)

Yugoslavia, like Bulgaria, has two climates, two religions, and two sorts of cuisine—both Eastern and Western. For five centuries the Turks occupied both these countries and brought with them Eastern dishes and Eastern ways. Most villages have still, beside their Slavic Orthodox churches, mosques for the Moslems. In the winter there are snow and sledges—a bitter cold Russian winter; and in the summer there is a dry, burning heat, often as hot as India. A typical dish from both Bulgaria and Yugoslavia is *sarma*. And in Russia the same thing is known as Muscovite Pigeon.

I was taught to make this by Raiina, my much-loved, never-to-be-forgotten Bulgarian maid, who could, when she chose, cook like an angel. When her black fits were on her, however, anything might arrive at table. She was of Macedonian origin, from a village near the Yugoslav border where feelings run high and each side of the frontier holds the other in scorn. During some of the time I lived in Sofia, political tension was acute. I could not pretend to understand Balkan politics, but we got quite used to Raiina rushing into the room brandishing a knife, and describing with graphic gestures just what she would do if she could lay her hands on a Serb. And when the cold wind howled down from the north, she would look out over the ring of snow-capped hills towards Yugoslavia . . . 'Serbski weather!' she would say, and spit, defiantly, as at the devil himself. But much must be forgiven those who have (politics apart) a loving heart. This Raiina had. She used to pad about the kitchen on large prehensile bare feet, her head bound in a bright handkerchief, never too tired (though she worked 18 hours a day, between my home and her own) to do anything asked of her. The kitchen was always filled with her family and friends, helping themselves from our larder. She used to lean out over the pastry-board and cuff her children, sometimes, for no apparent reason. 'Just to teach them not to start thinking up any mischief,' she would say, beaming fondly at the corrected infants.

When she herself had been particularly trying, she always knew how to wheedle herself back into my good graces. She would fetch one of the Gypsies from their quarter, the Mahalla, composed of straggling mud-huts and tinkers' booths, and get them to tell my fortune (gloriously), or show me how to cut the complicated *chalvari*, those draped Turkish trousers they all wore and which I coveted. Or she would arrange that one of the few remaining 'medicine bears' was hanging about outside, so that of course, enchanted, I had him fetched in. These bears, rather large brown ones, are trained to shuffle up and down the spine of anyone who dares to let them, thus giving a sort of tonic massage, highly beneficial, according to local opinion. Raiina herself favoured such a furry treatment, and when she felt low, or to brace her to cook a big dinner, she often had the bear in. These docile creatures shuffle and pad uneasily, a few paces forward, a few paces back, treading delicately along each side of the spinal cord. It seems to work wonders. Raiina always sprang up revivified. The only time I tried it I was too stiffened with terror to relax in the required manner, said Boris, the bear's owner. A glass of *slivovitz* (a plum brandy) was then ritualistically offered and drunk by all, the bear included. Raiina, whose sense of humour was robust, doubled up with laughter every time she told me how, once, a bear had been given too much to drink (they are partial to liqueurs) and his subsequent patients, Raiina's own brother among them, had to be treated in hospital. But back to cooking—*sarma* in particular.

½ cup sultanas
1 large cabbage
2 onions, chopped
Butter
½ cup uncooked rice
1 pound minced raw beef (or lamb or veal)
½ teaspoon salt
Pinch of pepper
½ tin tomato purée
2 tablespoons thick cream
1 cup yoghourt

Put ½ cup sultanas to soak in ½ cup hot water. Take a big cabbage with fine, untorn leaves. Plunge it into a large pot of boiling water to soften it. This is known as 'blanching' or 'parboiling'. Leave it in, about 10 minutes at most, then take it out, let it cool and drain. Then detach the leaves, cutting them from the hard centre, so that you have as many leaves as the *sarma* you may want to make—say 12, for 6 people. Chop up 2 onions and sauté them in a little butter for

5 minutes. Mix them with $\frac{1}{2}$ cup uncooked rice and 1 pound minced raw beef or lamb or veal. Add $\frac{1}{2}$ teaspoon salt, a pinch of pepper. Take the sultanas out of the hot water and add them. Mix all together very well.

Now comes the tricky part. Lay a cabbage leaf flat, put a heaping spoon of the meat mixture in the centre, and roll the cabbage leaf loosely around it, tucking in the sides like an envelope. Be sure to make the roll loose, because the rice will swell as it cooks. Tie each roll together with a piece of white thread. Lay them, one by one, very gently, for they split open easily, in a large dish or a saucepan. Pour one cup of warm water over them, cover the pot, and leave them to simmer (or cook very gently) for $\frac{1}{2}$ hour. Then finish them off with 10 minutes in a hot oven, still covered. Serve them with tomato sauce, which is easiest made if you heat a tin of tomato purée, add a squeeze of lemon and stir in 2 tablespoons of thick cream at the last moment. It is very soft and rich in taste. I like yoghourt served with them, as a second sauce.

DOLMAS (from all over the Near East and Turkey in particular)
(for 4)

Dolmas are really only stuffed vegetables. The most celebrated are cabbage leaves wrapping up meat, onion, and rice. (This is the *sarma* I have just described.) Perhaps the most delicious is the *dolma* made with specially prepared vine leaves, but once the basic meat stuffing is made, you can use it for many different vegetables, not necessarily the vine leaves, so difficult to get here.

You can fill cucumbers, small aubergines, or green peppers. (For the latter, remove seeds from your peppers first.) Cook these peppers or aubergines in boiling water for 15 minutes; cool, then cut off the tops and hollow them out with a teaspoon or grapefruit knife. Half fill all the vegetables with the stuffing. Then replace the tops, like a lid, lay them in a casserole (1 tablespoon oil and $1\frac{1}{2}$ cups water added) and cook in a medium oven for about 45 minutes.

In the case of cucumbers, peel, poach in salted water for 5 minutes; remove, scoop out seeds, having cut them in half lengthwise, fill the scooped out centres with (cooked) stuffing, and reheat, dabbed in butter, under the grill.

Here is a recipe for a meat filling for any *dolmas*.

Vine leaves (or cabbage leaves, cucumbers, aubergines, or green peppers)
1½ cups water
1 tablespoon oil
1 pound chopped meat (beef, veal or lamb)
2 chopped onions

½ cup rice (uncooked)
1 tablespoon tomato purée
Sprigs of parsley
Sprigs of mint
¼ cup pine kernels
Raisins
Salt and pepper

Take about 1 pound chopped meat, 2 coarsely chopped onions, ½ cup rice (uncooked), 1 tablespoon tomato purée, a few sprigs of parsley and mint, chopped fine, and if possible ¼ cup pine kernels, and some raisins. Mix all together, with salt and pepper to taste, and your stuffing is ready. This will stuff 8 large cucumbers or peppers or 4 medium aubergines.

Note.—Vine leaves can be bought in jars at certain progressive delicatessen shops, but not everywhere, alas! Chopped almonds can be used instead of pine kernels at a pinch.

MONK'S MACKEREL (from Greece)   (for 4)

Greece is surrounded by the most divinely beautiful islands. They are the home of many Greek legends, and when you see them rising out of the blue Aegean Sea you believe in Aphrodite and Apollo and Ulysses and all the immortals. One island, Mount Athos, the Holy Mountain, is a very strange place. It is filled with monasteries and monks. No woman is ever allowed to set foot on the island, and once no female animals were allowed, either. Only he-goats or mules; now they are a little less strict, and some monasteries permit female cats and chickens. There are no roads connecting the twenty different monasteries, which are often perched high on a rocky cliff, like a fortress, overhanging the sea. One of them can be reached only by a terrifying sort of basket, in which the visitor must sit and be pulled up inch by inch on jerking ropes, some hundreds of feet into the air. The pilgrims who visit this particular monastery, having spent all night in an open boat from Athens (on a sea not always

blue and calm), are said to regret their pious fervour sometimes until safety and the blessing of the Archimandrite is at last attained.

The monks wear long black robes, tall black hats, and never cut their hair or beards. Some of them paint beautiful frescoes on the walls of their churches; some cultivate the vegetables upon which they largely live; some work in the kitchens; and all of them spend many hours a day at prayer. It is a hard yet peaceful life. They look happy. Most of them eat well, though frugally. Fish, prepared all sorts of ways, is a staple food in Greece. This is how the monks cook mackerel, I was told by a friend who had stayed among them and who had watched Brother Timofei prepare them.

2 large or 4 small mackerel	Dash of pepper
2 onions, chopped	½ teaspoon salt
3 tablespoons olive oil	1 teaspoon dried mixed
2 bay leaves	herbs
3 lemons	12 black olives, stoned

Ask the fishmonger to split and clean the mackerel for you. Run cold water over them. Chop 2 small onions fine and fry them lightly in 1 tablespoon oil for about 3–4 minutes. Put 1 tablespoon olive oil in a flat baking dish. Lay the mackerel in the dish and sprinkle them with the fried onions, another tablespoon of oil, 2 bay leaves, the juice of a lemon, a dash of pepper, ½ teaspoon salt, and 1 teaspoon dried herbs. Put 12 stoned black olives all round, and cover the whole thing—if the dish has no cover of its own, you can use aluminium foil or greaseproof paper. Put the dish in a medium oven for ½ hour. Eat it with plain boiled potatoes; garnish with quarters of lemon.

THE MIDDLE EAST

KABUL RICE (from Afghanistan) (for 4)
(*The base of most Oriental dishes*)

I have not achieved Afghanistan in my wanderings, though I hope I may on my next journey, thus I cannot yet write about the food eaten there. The nearest I've been to it was an Afghan cook, found in a Turkish restaurant in New York, who spoke some English. He was very explicit about how to cook rice—it had to be left, warmly covered, beside the stove, for 12 hours. He led me into his kitchen and showed me a large copper bowl, snugly wrapped in a very dingy shawl—'my own', he said, proudly. But the whole process seemed unnecessarily complicated. My method, though not classic, usually achieves the dry fluffy rice essentially Eastern. Rice is the base of almost all Middle East cookery, and I cannot emphasize too strongly that it is *not* the rice we know in rice-pudding. Rice for a pilaff and most such dishes MUST BE DRY. Every grain should be fluffy and separate from its fellow grains. There are many ways of achieving this—and it *is* quite an achievement, as any experienced cook will agree. This is my way:

1 cup Patna rice	1 teaspoon salt
8–10 cups boiling water	

Boil up a big saucepan of water—the quantity need not be exact, as long as there is a lot—for 1 cup rice, say 8–10 cups water. Add 1 teaspoon salt. Wash the rice under cold running water, in a sieve, to remove the starch. As soon as the water boils furiously, put in your rice. Watch it carefully: as soon as the water begins to boil again (putting in the cold wet rice will stop the boiling), turn the heat low, and let it go on boiling gently for 13 minutes. No more, no less, and do not cover your saucepan. Then take it off, drain away the water by pouring the whole thing into a sieve or colander. Run cold water from the tap over the cooked rice for this will once again remove any starch left. Spread the rice out in a flat dish and put it into a medium oven to dry and reheat for 5 or 6 minutes. It should be white, dry, fluffy, and entirely right for a pilaff if you do all this exactly. Once you have mastered dry rice, you can make all sorts of Oriental dishes, adding eggs, shrimps, meat, onions, raisins, nuts—almost anything in fact.

THE SHAH'S PILAFF (from Iran) (for 6)

Iran, or Persia, as it used to be called, is a neighbour to Afghanistan, Pakistan, and Turkistan. It is beautiful, strange; 'the turquoise land' where there are inaccessible mountain ranges, historic buildings and gardens with fountain courts hidden behind high walls. In the main square of Isfahan, which is surrounded by the most lovely and graceful blue-tiled mosques, a turquoise blue which glitters against the deep blue sky, the Persians used to play polo and terrible Shahs are said to have used their enemy's head as a ball. Each successive

Shah inherited the splendid titles of his ancesters and was still King of Kings. His throne, said to contain parts of the legendary Peacock Throne of the Moguls, glittered with a fabulous collection of jewels. In the gold and mirror-inlaid palace at Teheran I once ate a pilaff which was first made by a celebrated cook called Nadir, who did it this way:

3 cups water
1 teaspoon salt
1½ cups long-grain rice
1 cup raisins
1 tablespoon grated orange rind
2 cups hot water
3 tablespoons sugar

1½ pounds lean beef or mutton
Oil
4 onions
1 cup stock or bouillon cube or water
¼ pound butter
Pinch of salt and pepper

Put 3 cups of boiling water and a pinch of salt in a bowl. Add 1½ cups long-grain rice. Let it simmer for a ½ hour. Meanwhile, soak a cup of raisins in 2 cups hot water and 3 tablespoons sugar. Take 1½ pounds meat, trimmed lamb best, cut it in cubes about 1 inch square. Sear them in a little oil. Set aside while you sauté 4 onions, coarsely chopped. Now put onion and meat in a casserole dish. Mix well together. Drain the water off the rice and the raisins and mix them, adding the grated orange rind. Spread on top of the meat and onions in a thick layer. Add 1 cup stock or water. Put 3 or 4 big chunks of butter, about ¼ of a pound at least, dotted about the top of the rice, and a pinch of salt and pepper. Put the whole thing in a medium oven, uncovered, for 30 to 40 minutes, Take a look at it once or twice. Stir 2 or 3 times so the top rice will not be hard. If the rice seems to be drying too fast, add ½ cup liquid bit by bit around the edges of the dish, and some more butter dabbed on top.

I expect those Kings of Kings, like their ancestors, followed this pilaff with some honeyed treat, perhaps walnuts cooked in honey, and little glasses of tea adorned with sprigs of mint.

FOUDJA DJEDAD (from Saudi-Arabia)   (for 4)

All over the East people like a mixture of sweet flavours with meat,
and fish too. Here is a simple, quick dish which combines apples and
chicken. They are very fond of this in the rich pearl merchants'
houses which fringe the Red Sea at ports such as Jeddah. Here the
Arab merchants sit bartering their pearls in the bright blue-painted
cafés along the waterfront. The pearl-divers hunt for pearls in the
depths of the ocean, and are sometimes themselves hunted by sharks.
It is a dangerous occupation.

Once Jeddah looked as if made of ivory, with creamy-coloured
carved and decorated houses (which were sometimes made of rough
coral) rising one above the other like card castles.

Yearly, the narrow streets are thronged with pilgrims from all
over the Moslem world, assembled there to begin their great
religious pilgrimage to Mecca. This is known as the *Hadj*; a man who
has done it is a *Hadji*, and has won the right to wear a green turban,
green being the sacred colour of Mohammed. Mecca is three days'
march inland across the burning hot desert. Camel and man take
their last rest and water in Jeddah. But, hidden away from all this,

behind high walls and latticed windows, live the women and children of Jeddah. The part of the house where they live unseen is the *harem*, or women's quarters. The women seldom go out. There is not much to do, except sleep, and eat, and gossip, tell fortunes, make mischief, or invent new ways to do their hair, or cook. *Foudja djedad* is one of their inventions.

This dish is appreciated all over the Levant. I first tried it in Beirut, where, in a house belonging to a Bedouin notable some Tunisian ladies I had first met on their way to Mecca, performing the *Hadj*, were now returning much fortified by the experience. Their descriptions of the latest means of transport, huge stream-lined, air-conditioned, American buses, in which the wealthier Faithful are conveyed painlessly across the dreaded, death-trap desert (two days' march between the wells, and each pilgrim carrying his own shroud) were so enthralling that I scarcely noticed what I ate. However, I was to meet this *Foudja djedad* again and again in the Near East, and later I found out its recipe.

4 large cooking apples	12 cloves
1 cup cooked chicken	Pinch of saffron
Salt and pepper	Pinch of cinnamon
½ cup breadcrumbs	Pinch of ginger
½ cup dried raisins	Brown sugar
2 tablespoons butter	Butter
1 cup mushrooms (optional)	Salt and pepper

Take as many *big* cooking apples as there will be people (2 for each person if they are very hungry). Core them, and scoop out some more of the apple so that a large hole is left in the middle. Do this very carefully or you will break the apples. Chop up pieces of a cooked chicken (no bones) or a tin of chicken meat (you should have at least 1 cup), mix with a little salt and pepper and about ½ cup breadcrumbs. This quantity will fill 6 big apples. Now add 2 tablespoons butter, about 12 cloves, a pinch of ginger, a pinch of cinnamon, and some chopped nuts. When this is well mixed together, fill the apples with it. Put a little brown sugar on the top of each one, and a big dab of butter. Put them in a baking dish (first covering the bottom with boiling water) and bake them in a medium oven, just as you would ordinary baked apples, for about ½ hour. Watch them, near the end of the half hour, to see they don't burst open, for then the stuffing would fall out and the dish be spoiled. The Syrian Arabs often end their meal with *mish-mish*, an apricot paste rolled thin, dried, and sold in flat pieces looking like shoe leather.

Another way to do the apples, if big, is to half cook them, before you stuff them, so that they are *thoroughly* cooked, in the shorter time it takes to cook their stuffing. I suggest serving plain boiled rice with the apples: but put a pinch of saffron in the water you cook the rice in. It will add a delicate colour and flavour.

MOUSSAKA (from Syria) (for 6)

This dish is one which is eaten a great deal in Turkey, but since the Turks were for many centuries rulers of so much of the Near East— their conquests stretching from Vienna to Egypt, by way of Syria and the Balkans, you will find *moussaka* being eaten in all eastern Europe and Asia Minor, and it is a very good way to make a little minced meat go a long way, say for a simple, economical party dish.

2 pounds minced beef or lamb	2 large onions
2 tablespoons water	2 large or 4 small tomatoes
2 tablespoons olive oil	Butter
1 medium aubergine	4 eggs
1 teaspoon salt	3 tablespoons flour
Olive oil for sauté	1 jar yoghourt
	Salt and pepper

Take 2 pounds minced meat, beef, or lamb. Sauté it lightly (about 5 minutes) in 2 tablespoons olive oil, breaking it apart with a fork as it cooks. You might add about 2 tablespoons water to the meat before you begin (mix it up in a bowl), as this will prevent it from becoming too dry in the frying pan. Take 1 nice plump, medium-sized aubergine, cut it in 1½-inch cubes, skin left on. Salt it, about 1 teaspoon sprinkled all over, and leave it to drain. The salt will draw out all the moisture. In ½ hour's time, rinse the salt off, dab roughly dry on a clean cloth, dust over with flour, and brown it in olive oil in a frying pan. Cut up coarsely 2 big onions and brown them, too. Last of all, leaving your other vegetables pushed to the side of the frying pan, cook 2 large or 4 small tomatoes, cut in thick slices, for about 5 minutes. They will take less time than the aubergine or onion. Butter a casserole and put in everything you have cooked, in layers: first meat, then aubergine, onions, and tomatoes, then more meat, then any vegetables left. Cook uncovered in a medium oven for ½ hour.

Now for the specially interesting part—the last touch that makes the true *moussaka*. Beat 4 eggs, blend in 3 tablespoons flour, add this to 1 jar of yoghourt to make a rich creamy yellow sauce, or else make it as you would a very soft batter-pudding. Add salt and pepper and pour this mixture over your casserole so that the meat and vegetables are thickly covered. Put it back in the oven for 15 minutes until the sauce is warmed right through and sets. By the way, it is generally held that you cannot cook yoghourt, that it disintegrates with heat. But I was taught by Erna, my Lithuanian maid, that the addition of a little flour makes the yoghourt quite manageable, and it can be usually used just as if it were cream.

Note.—If you cannot get aubergine, you can make a variation of *moussaka* with chunks of vegetable marrow, or large mushrooms.

THE EMIR'S JEWELS (from Trans-Jordan) (for 2)

I suppose this strange three-coloured salad got its name from some Arabian Nights tale of Aladdin in the magic cave discovering the robbers' horde of stolen gems, rubies, sapphires, emeralds, diamonds. Eastern people love jewels; they love them more for their colour and beauty than for their value. I knew a jewel merchant in Damascus who used to keep a handful of precious stones in his pocket, and as he talked he would bring them out and spill them over the table, playing with them, watching the light sparkling on them, and stroking them lovingly, as if they had been pets. He had one huge emerald to which he was especially attached because it reminded him of his sweetheart's eyes. He would never sell it however much he was offered. Occasionally he used to invite me to lunch with him, at the back of his shop in the *souk* (or bazaar), and his assistant used to come rushing in with a tray of tea, some rice and egg dish, and sometimes this bright, three-coloured, jewel-like salad, which I suggest you eat as an accompaniment to roast meat or chicken.

2 large onions	1 tablespoon salad oil
1 large orange	1 tablespoon lemon juice
1 green pepper	Salt, pepper, and mustard
12 black olives, stoned	$\frac{1}{2}$ teaspoon sugar

Peel and cut 2 large onions into very thin slices. Peel 1 large orange and cut it in thin slices. Take 1 large, bright green pepper, cut off the top and remove all the seeds and membrane. Cut it into the thinnest ring slices possible. Mix onions, oranges, and green peppers together in a flat dish and add about 12 black stoned olives. Make a dressing like this: 1 tablespoon salad oil, 1 tablespoon lemon juice, salt and pepper, a dash of mustard, and $\frac{1}{2}$ teaspoon sugar. Mix thoroughly and pour over the three-coloured salad. Serve as cold as possible.

BAALBEK APPLES (from the Lebanon)   (for 4)

This is not an Arab dish, but is said to have been invented by Lady
Hester Stanhope, niece of William Pitt, the great Prime Minister.
During his heyday she acted as his hostess, living a most worldly
and brilliant life. At his death in 1806, she retreated to live among
the Arabs of the Lebanon. She lived there alone with the tribes and
built a house high in the mountains, where, dressed as an Arab and
smoking the *tchibouk*, or water pipe, she used to receive her rare
European guests. I have heard that she gave them apples grown from
English seeds, but named after the ruined temple of Baalbek nearby.
This is how they are cooked.

2 pounds apples   1 tablespoon cinnamon
¼ pound butter   1 cup castor sugar

Choose eating apples, nice firm ones, about 2 pounds. Peel and
core them, and cut them in quarters. Melt about ¼ pound butter or
margarine, in a frying pan, and when smoking hot put in the apple
quarters. Use a spatula or a large flat knife to turn them carefully, so
they are thoroughly browned all over. Do them fast, on a high flame,
and take them out just the moment before they burn or begin to
turn black—this is tricky, but they are nicest when a tiny bit over-
cooked. Arrange them in a flat dish, side by side, and sprinkle them
with a mixture of castor sugar and cinnamon: 1 cup sugar to 1
tablespoon cinnamon.

SCHALÈTE (from Israel)

Many years ago the celebrated Jewish theatre group known as the
Habima Players came to London for a season, and I was then
reviewing plays and films, so that I went to see them in a critical
spirit. I found they offered some of the most magnificent evenings
in the theatre I have ever known, and I used to go night after night,

in neglect of all the other plays that were opening and closing-down elsewhere. In retrospect, the magic of such plays as *Uriel Acosta* or *The Dybbuk* still remains unchallenged; great theatre, great art. I came to know the troupe quite well, and when they were asked what they would especially like to do while in London, they chose an evening at the House of Commons. This was followed by an invitation to the Liberal Club, where, in an atmosphere redolent of over-stuffed leather chairs and dominated by busts of Mr. Gladstone and other pillars of Liberalism, the Habima Players settled down to an evening's pleasure among a number of club members who seemed not to know whom they had in their midst, and who were far too well-bred to ask. Later, the actors gave a small party, themselves, on the stage after a performance, and I remember they regretted not being able to offer their guests the sort of traditional Jewish dishes they would have provided had they been in Israel. But all the same, they achieved a splendid *Schalète*, an apple and raisin cake, and here it is.

1 breakfast cup of stale breadcrumbs	2 pounds apples
	1 teacup raisins
2½ breakfast cups of white sugar	6 eggs
	½ wineglass rum

Put the breadcrumbs to soak in boiling water in a big basin; soak the raisins in the rum. Peel and core the apples and chop them into very small pieces. Drain off any water not absorbed by the bread-crumbs. Add to the (now soggy) breadcrumbs your apples, sugar, and the raisins and rum, and mix all together thoroughly. Now add, one by one, stirring all the while, your six eggs, and add a pinch of salt. Butter (sides and bottom) a deep dish that has a lid, and is also fireproof—an enamel or fireproof glass is best. Heat it till the fat smokes, then powder the inside with sugar, so the sides of the dish are coated thickly. Fill with the mixture, pack it down tightly, and put on the lid. Heat it on a fast stove for about 7–10 minutes, then put it in a very slow oven, for about 2 hours. Let it get cold gradually (not in the refrigerator) and turn it out (upside down) to serve. You might add a hot rum sauce or rum-flavoured cream; or a honey sauce, or even one made of the smoky-flavoured maple syrup beloved of American cooks. Served so, with an important sauce, it becomes less cakey, more of a sweet.

AFRICA

TCHAK-TCHOUKA (from Tunisia)   (for 6)

On the tiny, toylike island of Djerba, off the coast of southern
Tunisia, there is an even more toylike small town—Houmt-Souk,
the capital. There, as all along the Tunisian coast, you find blue-
painted cafés where the Arabs gather at dusk bringing with them their
songbirds to take a lesson from the master songbird, owned by the
café proprietor. A really melodious songster is invaluable to the
café, attracting more clients than anything else. The men sit drinking
their little glasses of green tea, talking quietly, often with a spray of
jasmine held in the hand, or a rose tucked over one ear, for they
are passionately devoted to perfumes; beside them on the tables are
small cages made of porcupine quills, in which the pupil birds have
been brought to take their lesson. The master songbird is probably
housed in a spacious, elaborately fretted metal cage, painted blue
and shaped like a pavilion, domed or turreted; such cages are a
speciality of this region—some of the most beautiful being made from
old sardine tins. There are few restaurants at Houmt-Souk—a street
booth offers grilled fish, and a local delicacy (*brique*), a sort of folded
puff pastry, concealing a poached egg, and most difficult to eat
neatly. The *brique* vendors used to sit cross-legged, perched up on a
high tiled shelf beside the cauldron of smoking hot fat. I used to rush
out, very early, to buy *briques* for my breakfast, while all around me,
Houmt-Souk woke to another day of blueness, of trotting donkeys
bringing in the baskets of octopus, or sponges, of camels loaded with
clay water-jars, of blind fortune tellers chanting their prophecies,
of snake-charmers and musicians from the Sudan, all gathering
under the palms and arcades of the market place . . . those were
mornings in Paradise . . .

Over on the mainland, in a mysterious little-known region called
the Mhatmata, the inhabitants live in caves and you go down ladders
into a kind of red earth pit round which the cave opens. I was sometimes lucky enough to be invited to share the family meal. *Tchak-
tchouka* was a favourite dish. I used to sit on the red mud floor of the
pit and watch the women, in their blue robes hung with amulets
and lucky charms, preparing this, or a *couss-couss* (a sort of semolina

and meat dish), but since that is very complicated to do out of Africa, I will concentrate on the *tchak-tchouka*.

5 or 6 large onions	1 clove garlic, chopped (optional)
Oil	
5 or 6 large tomatoes	Pinch of paprika (optional)
3 green peppers	6 eggs (1 for each serving)
Sweet red pimentos	

Slice 5 or 6 large onions rather thin and brown them in oil. Then add the same quantity of very large tomatoes, sliced, 3 finely chopped green peppers, and a few sweet red pimentos. Don't forget to cut open the green peppers and remove all the seeds first. Cook all of the vegetables together slowly in the frying pan until they are a soft pulpy mass. Then add a clove of garlic, chopped, if you like, and maybe a pinch of paprika. Now put the mixture into separate earthenware dishes, one for each person; break an egg on top of each, and put in a low oven until the egg is just set (about 10 minutes). I don't know how you will like this; but I loved it, as I sat among my Arab friends in the evening twilight, and the huge stars shone in the greenish sky, while the camels tethered to the palms above groaned and snorted for their own dinner—nothing nearly so nice.

MECHOUI
(Roast lamb, from all the Arab countries, and particularly North Africa)

Roast lamb, roasted whole on a spit, is a delicacy in every Arab country. Sometimes it is basted with honey or stuffed with raisins; often it is eaten with a yoghourt sauce, which is how I used to eat it in Syria. But whether you are among the Bedouins of Syria or the nomad tribes of the Sahara, or enjoying the hospitality of an Arab noble-man's family (as you see me doing in the sketch, where I am talking to some of the wives on the roof in the cool of the evening), the ritual of the feast remains the same. Most probably you will not eat with the women. They will prepare the feast, but it is your host, his sons and brothers with whom you will dine. Your host will offer you, in his fingers, the greatest delicacy, the sheep's eye, which he will dig out of the surrounding meat and rice, and you must not refuse or seem less than enchanted, or it would hurt everyone's feelings.

I recall a supper to which some French Army officers took me, when we were all invited by a princely Arab in the desert. The men were sitting outside their black goat's-hair tents in the dusk, the firelight flickering over them—tall, dark, bearded men, most of them. They had been out hunting gazelle; their horses were picketed nearby. The chief's son had a favourite white stallion which had its mane and tail dyed a rosy apricot colour, with henna—the same greenish powder that is used to tint the palms of the hand and the feet in most Eastern countries, and for auburn hair dye here. (Alas! on the hands and feet it soon turns to a dingy brown, and is not as beautiful as the poets would have us believe.) We joined the circle round the fire, and I saw that some of the hunters still had their falcons (the birds they use in hunting) perched on their shoulders, and sometimes they spoke to them and petted them. Meanwhile, beyond the circle of firelight the women were preparing our supper, boiling water for the mint tea, baking flat loaves in clay and ash ovens, and patting goat's cheese into little squares, while the *mechoui* was turned slowly on its spit. Of course, you cannot cook meat in this way on a kitchen stove, but here are some suggestions for good roasting, which is pretty much the same all the world over.

If you like the flavour of garlic, peel 2 small cloves, make a slit in the leg of lamb here and there and insert tiny slivers of garlic. Rub the meat all over with a little salt. Put a couple of tablespoons of oil or butter in your roasting pan and turn your meat in this, once or twice, before you begin to cook it.

There is one great secret for good roasting. Sear, or seal the meat first by 10 or 15 minutes of high heat (oven preheated). Then, when the juices are sealed in and the outside is a lightish brown, diminish the heat considerably, and continue to roast in a moderate oven. You must calculate 15 to 20 minutes for each pound. Thus, a 5-pound leg of lamb (which will feed 6 people) must be cooked about 1 hour and 45 minutes if you like it rather well done. To my mind underdone lamb is as disagreeable as overdone beef.

To make a good gravy, follow the recipe on page 170. I like to serve yoghourt as sauce, in the Arab way. English mint sauce is good, too. You can add potatoes or onions (first parboiled 15 minutes) all around the meat, and roast them with it, basting them with its gravy. (If you don't parboil them first they won't be ready when the meat is done.) Very good indeed, and economical, for everything cooks in one dish.

BAMYIA-FIGS (from Egypt)   (for 4)

In Egypt the very rich eat very richly, while the very poor, the *fellahs* as they are called, eat very poorly. Once a year, rich or poor alike keep a curiously named celebration, 'Smell-the-Breezes Day', when nothing is eaten, and the spring air is considered as good as a feast. Outside the city of Cairo the desert begins at once, with its great Pyramids and the Sphinx, which every newcomer, from Napoleon to a one-day tourist, hurries to see. Cairo is full of splendours and legends. The greatest religious university in the Moslem world is there, at the Mosque El Azhar. The island of Roda, on the Nile, is where, they say, Pharaoh's daughter found Moses in the bulrushes. Above all, there are the tombs of the Mamelukes, that extraordinary band of mercenaries who were once Turkish or Georgian slaves. Sold to a Sultan of Egypt, they presently overthrew him to become a powerful ruling dynasty—the Mameluke Sultans—who remained in power for several hundred years. The last of them were destroyed by Mehemet Ali.

Cairo has many such echoes, still to be heard, sometimes, in the great bazaars, the roofed-in winding alleys full of merchandise: leather, ostrich feathers and the giant eggs, too; rugs, sugar, beautifully coloured printed cottons manufactured in England, and the treasures of the Pharaohs, both genuine and false, for the Egyptians are good businessmen and order large quantities of well-copied antiques for the tourist market. In the bazaars, there are a lot of little cafés, where bargaining is carried on for hours: this bartering is an indispensable part of Eastern life. A sale often takes all day and is interspersed with several cups of coffee, and even a meal. At the restaurants in the bazaar you will find delicious dishes, shrimps and cuttle-fish, very sweet cakes, honeyed delights, and many vegetable dishes. One of the favourites is *bamyia* (or Ladies' Fingers), which we know as okra, eaten hot or cold, as a salad. I prefer it hot, with garlic, and a sour-cream sauce, made sharper by adding lemon juice.

8 fresh figs	Brown sugar
1 pound okra or 8 small courgettes or 2 pounds runner or broad beans	Salt and black pepper Yoghourt
2 ounces butter	Parsley

Bamyia, or okra, is cooked in Egypt very much as we cook it here, when we can get it. The dried sort is sometimes to be found in foreign delicatessen shops. If you cannot find it, use tiny courgettes or even runner beans. In Egyptian restaurants I have eaten *bamyia* cooked in a casserole together with fresh figs treated as a vegetable. Plunge the fresh okra in salted boiling water and let it simmer for about 30 minutes. (1 pound of okra is enough for 4 people.) When soft, remove, drain, and combine with a dish of figs which are cooked in a casserole, with a little butter, salt, and pepper, in a medium oven for about 15 minutes. Arrange the figs and vegetables together, sprinkle lightly with brown sugar, and put under the grill just long enough for the sugar to caramelize. Serve with melted butter or yoghourt as an accompaniment to any meat dish. If eaten as a main course, I suggest it be accompanied by poached eggs or with plenty of grated cheese sprinkled over it, and tomato sauce on the side.

Bamyia are very good served with broad beans, too. Put the beans in boiling salted water, 1 pound beans to ½ cup water; simmer slowly till tender, about 30 minutes. Add a sprinkle of chopped parsley and a dab of butter. Serve them with the Ladies' Fingers in neat, separate heaps on the dish, and decorate with quarters of lemon, and maybe a few black olives, for beauty's sake. So much of the success of a dish can depend on how it is presented—garnished —or arranged on the plate. Oriental cooks are very good at this. It is worth taking some trouble over it. The best cooking, if just thrown on a plate, is not tempting. And, in the same way, the plainest food, prettily arranged, with some unexpected extra, put there either for a surprise flavour *or just for the colour or coolness and freshness it brings*, such as quarters of lemon, or red radishes or parsley, or shiny black olives—all help to create an air of fine cooking.

CONGO CHICKEN (from Equatorial Africa)   (for 4)

In the steamy forests of central Africa, right on the Equator, there are all sorts of tropical fruits, pawpaws, mangoes, and bananas. The natives eat these, with chicken, eggs, and rough maize or corn meal biscuits and a porridgy mush. Bananas cooked many ways are the principal food. Ostrich eggs are a great treat; they are far too large to eat except when beaten into a sort of omelette, one making a substantial dish for about 6 people. Sometimes there are feasts with elephant meat. If you were to paddle down one of the yellow, swirling rivers, you would see the hippos mudbathing on the banks and the crocodiles basking in the sun, their huge ugly mouths held open, so that little birds can hop about and pick their teeth clean of meat. I know this sounds unlikely, but it is true: the birds follow the hippos and crocodiles about and get their food this way, while the crocodiles never snap at the tooth-pick birds who are so helpful.

If your canoe were to steer up one of the little creeks which lead inland to a village, a great silence would fall; the forest would close in, thick, steamy, green, silent, with only the rustle of a bird or the slither of some snake in the undergrowth. Perhaps you would hear a faraway crashing and snapping, as a herd of elephants stamped through the undergrowth. They sometimes come to the villages, because they like to eat the sort of shrub often used to fence the houses, and are usually chased off by noise, banging tins and

shouting. On the whole, they are peaceable, but very obstinate, and terrifying if angry.

The African villages are cheerful, busy places, full of life, children darting about, scrawny chickens pecking in the dust, and old crones preparing food in rough clay ovens outside each hut. If they invited you to join them at a feast they might give you chicken cooked something like this, though I doubt they would have butter, and green peppers are my substitute for purely local vegetables.

1 3-pound chicken	Oil
¼ pound butter	Peanut butter
Salt	1 cup roasted peanuts,
6 green peppers	unsalted

Take a 3-pound chicken, cleaned and prepared for roasting: now pack the inside with ¼-pound butter and a handful of peanuts. Rub the chicken all over with salt and dabs of butter. Put in a medium oven and roast. The length of time depends on its weight: reckon 20 minutes to the pound. Thus a 3-pound chicken needs just about 1 hour. Baste it occasionally.

Meanwhile, take 6 green peppers and cook them whole, very fast, for 10 minutes, in a frying pan and very little oil. Let them get a bit burned, or blackened, outside. Take them off the fire, allow to cool slightly, cut off the tops, scoop out the centres, cut the rest in strips, and put in the oven around the chicken, spooning a little of the butter the chicken is cooking in over them. Baste again when the chicken is half done. When your chicken is tender (prod the leg with a fork to see), take it out of the oven, spread it all over, rather thinly, with peanut butter. Salt it. Now take a cupful of chopped or coarsely ground roasted peanuts and sprinkle them all over your chicken. They will stick to the peanut butter and form a prickly-looking nutty coating. Put back in the oven and cook for another 5 or 6 minutes. Then serve surrounded by the green peppers. Eat plain rice with this into which, at the last moment, you have sprinkled finely chopped fresh green parsley.

As a sweet, mangoes would be classically correct, but difficult to obtain. Try bananas, peeled, split lengthwise, with the juice of a lemon squeezed over them, and a dusting of brown sugar, heated in the oven for 10 minutes. By the way, if you overcook them—say 25–30 minutes, they puff up into a sort of purée-soufflé, quite an agreeable dish, which, however, tends to be insipid unless accompanied by a tart sauce. I often make one of *bitter* marmalade, heated, and thinned with a tot of dark rum and a little lemon juice and brown sugar.

THE FAR EAST

THE ROSY DAWN DISH (from Indonesia)   (for 4)

It is curious to see how, all over the world, the same ideas in food are repeated in different countries. Bananas with fish and tomatoes eaten together, are found all along the Eastern Mediterranean, particularly in Spain, and we find fish with banana widely eaten in the Orient too.

Here is something which is extremely pretty when well arranged. It looks best on a green dish, or surrounded by big green leaves. In the East people often serve food on shells instead of plates, or on the huge shiny tropic leaves which grow everywhere. However, we can find some sort of substitute: try curly kale or large, fresh, bloomy cabbage leaves, or the beautiful red-veined leaves of rhubarb, said to be poisonous if eaten, but no doubt harmless as a platter.

1 quart water
1 teaspoon salt
1 cup rice
4 eggs, hard-boiled
4 small ripe tomatoes
1 package frozen cooked shrimps, thawed or 1 jar cocktail shrimps or some fresh prawns

2 tablespoons oil
1 tablespoon lemon juice
Salt and pepper
Paprika
3 ripe bananas
$\frac{1}{4}$ cup tomato purée
$\frac{1}{4}$ cup mayonnaise
Butter (if served as hot dish)

This is an excellent main dish for a buffet supper. (Start off with cups of scalding hot bouillon, though.) It can be eaten hot or cold. Let us say we will have it cold. Cook the rice as for a pilaff, p. 89, for just 13 minutes. Let it cool. Meanwhile, hard-boil 4 eggs (8 minutes), slice some tomatoes thin, about 4 big, ripe ones. Now take a package of frozen shrimps, or a large jar of big cocktail shrimps, and turn them several times in a mixture of 2 tablespoons oil and 1 of lemon juice, with salt and pepper and a pinch of paprika added. Leave them to soak in this while you cut up 3 rather ripe bananas, lengthwise and then across, so that you have 12 pieces; sprinkle them with salt, pepper, and a little paprika. Shell the eggs and cut in half, lengthwise. Now put your cold rice in the centre of a flat dish, and arrange alternate shrimps, banana slices, and eggs all around. Make an outer ring of sliced tomatoes; in the centre of the rice, scoop out a place to sink a glass bowl of sauce: ¼ cup tomato purée, thinned out with ½ cup of mayonnaise; it should be a lovely shrimp pink colour. (Of course if you make this a hot dish, you must lightly sauté the bananas, tomatoes, and shrimps in butter before serving.) Finish by sprinkling the rice with powdered sweet paprika. Serve a sweet relish or pickle as an extra.

HONOURABLE STRANGER'S CHOP SUEY (from China)
(for 4)

Chinese cooking can be as poetic and as lovely as Chinese painting, in spite of all the stories of two-hundred-year-old eggs, monkeys' brains, and mice. It is considered one of the great triumphs of gastronomy, but the ingredients and methods used are especially hard to translate. Vegetables, spices, all sorts of specialties, belong to the Chinese menu which New Yorkers and San Franciscans can find in various degrees of excellence in their respective Chinatowns. And on Long Island outside New York there are whole farms and vegetable gardens where the special Chinese ingredients are cultivated, usually by Chinese-American families. Restaurants achieve fine results; but I don't think the amateur European cook is so lucky, as a rule. However, with rice, pork, shrimps, mushrooms, soy sauce, and a tin of bean or bamboo shoots, you can get something rather like a Chinese dish and the Chinese people are so polite they will always tell you it is better than they could do. Remember that the most celebrated Chinese dish, chop suey, means, literally, 'any old bits,' so that it is possible to make a very fair imitation of it, and at the same time use up left-overs or scraps. Try this recipe:

1 cup cooked meat (left-overs such as pork, chopped ham, chicken liver, or chicken meat)
Salt and pepper
2 tablespoons vinegar
2 tablespoons water
1 cup raw mushrooms
2 onions
1 tin bean sprouts (or bamboo sprouts)
Soy sauce
1 teaspoon sugar
Pinch of allspice
Dish of cooked long-grain rice
$\frac{1}{2}$ pound boiled shrimps
Butter

Let us suppose you have a few pieces of cooked pork. Cut them into small cubes. Add a few pieces of chopped ham, chicken meat . . . almost anything you have will do. You need about 1 cup of meat altogether. Put it aside, with pepper and salt sprinkled over it, and 2 tablespoons each of vinegar and water. Leave it to soak. Add 1 cup raw mushrooms, cut up, to soak with it. Peel 2 onions, chop coarsely, and sauté in butter. Now take a tin of bean sprouts or bamboo sprouts (if you cannot get these try thin slices of celery, or French beans, cooked in boiling water for only about 5 minutes) and sauté these, too, in butter, for about 2 minutes. Now add your meat and mushrooms and cook for 3 minutes more. Add 1 teaspoon soy sauce, 1 teaspoon sugar, and a pinch of allspice. Cook all together over low heat for 15 minutes. Meantime, you have prepared a big dish of white long-grain rice, as for a pilaff (page 89). Serve rice and chop suey in separate bowls. Then add $\frac{1}{2}$ pound boiled shrimps to your fried mixture, at the last, and cook them about 1 minute with the rest. Serve a side dish of soy sauce and a sweet relish.

No, Chinese cooking is neither quick nor simple, by our standards.

PEKIN PEARS (from China)   (for 4)

Alas! I have never seen Jehol, or the Forbidden City, or the Great Wall stretching to infinity. This is one of the deep regrets of my life. I have come no nearer to them than reading the travels of the

Jesuit fathers, Huc and Gabet, who have left such an enthralling account of their journey through Tartary, China, and Tibet in 1842, when they set out to visit the Chinese Christians of Mongolia. Anything I know of Chinese food is limited to restaurant meals, the best being in San Francisco's Chinatown, where the shops are filled with shark's fins, dried duck, and unnameable roots and vegetables. There you will hear Chinese spoken all round you, and every night there is the Chinese Opera, traditional dramas that last twelve hours or so (shortened versions of the real thing) with little bowls of tea and rice, and steaming hot towels passed round among the spectators, to refresh them, throughout the performance. True, chewing-gum and Coca-Cola are also obtainable for the more Americanised young Chinese, but the whole spectacle, the brilliant mediaeval costumes, the masklike make-up, the ritualistic gestures, and high fluted voices are all Asia. Around midnight, I used to wander out to eat in a little restaurant nearby, choosing one of the classic dishes, and perhaps Pekin Pears to follow. There are very few desserts eaten in China. A sort of fruit soup, or little rice cakes, or chunks of preserved ginger, or some exotic fruit, like *lychee* which you can buy tinned, is served. (Milk is considered altogether unfit for human consumption, by the way.) An old Chinese way to prepare pears is as follows.

4 pears	1 tablespoon chopped
4 tablespoons honey	walnuts
Ginger	

The pears are peeled and cored, so that they have a hole right through the centre. This is filled with honey, chopped walnuts, and a little powdered ginger. The pears are then either baked in a very slow oven, $\frac{3}{4}$ hour at least, or steamed for even longer, till tender. Be sure you choose fairly ripe pears. Very green, hard ones would not be good, though you could use up not quite ripe ones this way. They become soft and most deliciously flavoured though the time they take depends on the fruit. I cannot be precise.

BLACK AND WHITE SALAD (from Japan) (for 4)

In those remote days before the industrialisation of Japan, the country looked like a screen by Koyetsu, with ferocious warriors brandishing swords. Koyetsu came of a family of sword-makers—the sword being a cult, in Japanese tradition. There were proud nobles dallying with graceful, fabulously dressed women, humble peasants, fantastically plumed birds and strange fish, and perhaps more legends and superstitions there than anywhere else. Every day, event, emotion, flower, animal, or person was linked with some aspect of the fabulous. When the Samurai—one of the class of hereditary warriors—left his home to follow his lord and master to the wars, it was the custom for his household to serve him a special farewell dish—a baked *tai*, or perch, which had to be served up on a big leaf of the *tegashiwa* shrub. The leaf was then hung over the door, as a spell, to ensure the Samurai's safe return. The Japanese eat a lot of fish and rice—the fish is usually raw. Their food is less easy for us to appreciate than that of the Chinese, and more difficult to find here. But the few Japanese restaurants I have visited all have this Oriental gift for making the most of little and of presenting their dishes beautifully. As I have said before, this is very important. Here is a curious sea-food salad, which is easy to do with ordinary ingredients.

4–6 left-over boiled potatoes   Pinch of dill
2 tablespoons white wine   Mace
    vinegar   About 15 mussels (or 1 tin)
Juice ½ small lemon   ¼ pound button mushrooms
Salt and pepper   (or one tin)
Parsley (a large handful)   Walnut halves

Slice 4 to 6 cold, left-over boiled potatoes, let them marinate or soak in the following mixture: 2 tablespoons white wine vinegar, juice of half a small lemon, salt and pepper, and a large handful of coarsely chopped parsley. Add a pinch of dill, and a very little powdered mace. Now drain a tin of cooked mussels and a tin of cooked button mushrooms. Mix mushrooms, mussels, and potatoes together gently, so as not to mash them. Garnish the mixture with a few walnut halves, and serve if possible in a bright-coloured bowl— a much prettier setting than glass, or white china, in this case.

A CURRIED RICE DISH (from India)   (for 4)

Very hot climates seem to produce very hot dishes. Perhaps people get so exhausted they need a shock to enjoy their food. Curry is a good example of this sort of strongly flavoured dish. A really perfect curry should be so strong that it brings tears to the eyes of the Westerner. Traditionally it should be accompanied by a sort of flat, wrinkled dried fish, known as Bombay Duck, and milk is drunk with it, I suppose to cool off. Personally I do not like so strongly flavoured a dish; but curry used in very small quantities is delicious, so let us make a much more delicate, gentle, westernized curried rice.

1 cup rice	1 tablespoon flour
8 cups water	2 tablespoons milk
3 teaspoons curry powder	Salt and pepper
Raisins (a handful)	1 teaspoon Worcester sauce
2 tablespoons sugar	Curry powder
2 apples	Pinch of powdered ginger
2 medium onions	Pinch of dry mustard
Butter	Chutney or sweet pickles
4 eggs, hard-boiled	

Cook 1 big cup rice in about 8 cups water and 1 teaspoon curry powder. Let it cook without a lid on the saucepan for 15 minutes. Meanwhile, put a handful of raisins to soak in a cup of hot water and 2 tablespoons sugar. Slice 2 large cooking apples and 2 medium-sized onions fine and sauté in butter till they are rather dark brown, and while all this is going on hard-boil 4 eggs (8 minutes).

By now your rice should be done; pour off the curried water into a bowl (you'll need some of it for the sauce). Let your rice, which will have turned a bright yellow, drain well. Then mix into it your browned slices of onion and apple and your raisins. Put the whole dish into a very low oven to keep warm, though not to go on cooking. In a cup mix 1 tablespoon flour with 2 tablespoons the curry water; mix well until the flour dissolves. Add 2 tablespoons milk; mix well, and put it in a saucepan over low heat, and add gradually, stirring all the while, ½ cup curry water. Add salt, pepper, 1 teaspoon Worcestershire sauce, another ¼ teaspoon curry powder, a pinch of powdered ginger, and a pinch of dry mustard. When the sauce thickens, it is done.

Now peel your eggs. They will be too hot to handle at first, so dip them in cold water till you can remove the shells. Slice in half lengthwise, and put them all round your dish of curried rice. Serve with it your curry sauce, and some sweet pickle or chutney.

An Imperialistic Postscript

Or, as a souvenir of Anglo-India, try Simla Chicken.

Roast chicken, cut up, put in the oven in a fireproof dish, covered in a sauce made of 1 cup whipped cream, 1 teaspoonful of mustard, 3 tablespoons Worcester sauce, salt and pepper, a dash of cayenne, a teaspoon of ginger. Pour over the chicken and brown in oven. Serve with curry flavoured rice.

KHOA (from Pakistan)   (for 4)

1 pint cream cheese	Flour
2 tablespoons sour cream	Butter
1 tablespoon sugar	Brown sugar

If you want to have an all-Indian meal, you could finish with *khoa*. For this, take a pint of cream cheese and mix it with 2 tablespoons sour cream and 1 tablespoon sugar. Shape it into little cakes, dust with flour, sauté in butter or oil, and serve sprinkled with brown sugar. With this, maybe, some peaches or grapes. A noble dessert, fit for the splendours of a Maharajah such as I have drawn here. (And far better than 'Flannel Rolls', a dubious joy given

in *The Mem-Sahib's Cake Book*; this sternly practical affair has weights and measures in Hindustani, 4 chittocks of flour, 1 passeree of oatmeal, and such. It was published in India in 1857, the year of the Mutiny, so that perhaps buns as well as the alleged greased bullets were a contributing factor.)

THE PACIFIC

PINEAPPLE PIGEON (from any South Sea Island)   (for 2)

There is an old saying that you cannot eat pigeon every day of your
life. But why should you? Still, one man did actually bet another
that he could do so, by cooking it in different ways, every day
for a year. He started off gaily; he was a fine cook, and he prepared
his daily pigeon in many disguises. After about three months, the
other man began to get rather anxious. It was a big bet and he feared
he would lose. But presently, after six months or so, the pigeon-eater
suddenly began to look sickly; next, he fell ill—so ill he could not
be cured till he gave up and agreed to eat all sorts of other things
besides pigeons. Although he lost the bet, he regained his health.
This is a true story, but it has absolutely no moral; still, it is a fact
that you can't eat pigeon every day of the year, as you can bread or
milk. Anyhow, once in a while pigeon is delicious. You might try it
the way they eat it in the South Sea Islands.

Ever since Robinson Crusoe, Captains Cook and Bligh, the Swiss
Family Robinson, and the boy and girl made famous in *The Blue
Lagoon* lived such adventurous lives on tropical islands, we have a
mental picture of their being nourished on fruit and fish, both raw.
We know they did cook, but it is difficult to imagine them spending

much time over the cauldron when all those coral reefs and blue lagoons and coconut groves were waiting to be explored. Yet the most succulent dishes have originated in the various Pacific Islands. Roast pork with coconut, or breadfruit with fish is typical. A French friend of mine ate pigeon casserole when he was sailing about those blue, blue waters visiting Samoa, the island home of Robert Louis Stevenson, and Tahiti, where that uncomfortable genius, Paul Gauguin, went to live and paint his beautiful pictures, and, at last to die.

This is the recipe my French friend brought me from the South Seas.

2 pigeons
Oil
Salt and pepper
Powdered ginger
1 cup water and 1 table-
   spoon lemon juice

2 or 3 bay leaves
1 or 2 pieces fennel
1 teaspoon grated nutmeg
2 thick slices fresh pineapple
Mustard

Take 2 pigeons, rub them over with oil, sprinkle with a little salt and pepper and a little powdered ginger (very little). Put them in a casserole with 1 cup water and 1 tablespoon lemon juice. Add 2 or 3 bay leaves and a couple of pieces of fennel, chopped fine. Grate 1 teaspoon nutmeg and add to this. Cut a couple of thick slices of fresh pineapple. (Tinned fruit is a poor substitute, but if you must use it get the unsweetened kind). Cut off the prickly outside and remove the hard core. Cut the fruit into finger lengths and arrange this around the pigeons. Cook the casserole, covered, for at least an hour, in a slow oven. Serve with sweet potatoes, or mashed potatoes, or jerusalem artichokes, which go admirably with this dish. A daring but pleasing addition is pineapple treated as a vegetable. Use the fresh or unsweetened tinned kind, cut into cubes and lightly fry in butter.

And the Hawaiian meals I have enjoyed are always accompanied by a violent mustard sauce: mix a saucerful of cream, a dessertspoon of powdered mustard and a teaspoon of sugar, or honey.

BARLEY MUTTON (from New Zealand)   (for 4)

Australia has fine fruits, all sorts of fish, koala bears—though of course these are not eaten, but very much petted, for they are droll, lovable little creatures. There are gardens full of oleanders, camelias, and deadly snakes; there are also endless plains where some of the greatest sheep-raising stations are found. Mutton, then, is a regular food in both Australia and New Zealand—but it is not eaten in the same sort of ways as in the Arab countries with rice or raisins or yoghourt. In New Zealand it is generally prepared in a much more simple way, for far out on the sheep farms life is hard and there is little time for elaborate cooking. This is a straightforward, very good way of preparing a lamb or mutton stew.

8 small lamb or mutton chops	3 tablespoons pearl barley
4 cups water	6 carrots
Lemon peel	4 onions
	Salt and pepper

Take 8 small loin or neck, lamb or mutton chops. Put them in a saucepan with 4 cups water, a little lemon peel, 2 tablespoons pearl barley, 6 carrots cut in quarters, and 4 medium onions cut in half. Add plenty of salt and pepper. Cover, and simmer very slowly for 2 hours. Eat with potatoes, if you are hungry, though the barley will thicken the gravy and be quite a sustaining addition.

To follow, I would suggest a ginger cake, with sour cream to which you have added a little sugar and powdered ginger to taste (go easy on this). I suggest this rather hot-flavoured dessert to follow the Barley Mutton because the mutton is very delicately flavoured, and the ginger makes a nice sharp contrast. If you want something lighter, then serve fruit (but not a compôte), melon, perhaps, with powdered ginger and sugar to give it zest.

AMBROSIA (from Hawaii)   (for 6)

On the dreamy song-filled island of Hawaii, feasts are as celebrated as hula dances and guitar music. Sucking pig—a baby piglet roasted whole—is one of the usual dishes. Since every sort of tropic fruit abounds, the people of Hawaii make fruit salads that are superlatively good. Here is one, and a pretty way to serve it too.

1 very large fresh pineapple	Fresh white cherries, stoned
2 oranges	Fresh strawberries or
2 fresh pears	raspberries
1 cup seedless white grapes	4 tablespoons sugar
$\frac{1}{2}$–$\frac{3}{4}$ cup sliced peaches, frozen or fresh	Juice of 2 lemons
	Grated coconut (optional)

First, cut a very large pineapple in half lengthwise, right through the stem: be sure it is a fruit with fine, unbroken leaves, as this will be part of the decoration. With a sharp knife cut out the hard centre from each half and throw it away. Next, cut out the flesh carefully (a grapefruit knife is good for this) leaving a thin layer of it next to the prickly husk. Save the shells.

On a plate cut the flesh you have taken out into small cubes, or wedges, and put the juice left in the plate aside in a cup. Now get a big bowl and begin mixing your Ambrosia, or fruit salad. You can use most fruits. Try this mixture: 2 oranges, peeled and cut in thin rounds, the rounds then cut in half again; 2 fresh pears, peeled and cut in small chunks; 1 cup of white grapes; $\frac{1}{2}$–$\frac{3}{4}$ cup frozen or fresh peach slices; a few white cherries, stoned; your pieces of pineapple, and a few raspberries or strawberries. Mix all together, so as not to break the fruit, adding at least 4 tablespoons sugar. Pour over it the juice of 2 lemons and some of the juice of the fresh pineapple that was put by. Leave the whole thing in the refrigerator for some hours to chill properly.

To serve, spoon the fruit salad into the empty pineapple shells, arranged on a large platter side by side, top to toe—that is, the leaves of one at one end of the dish, the others at the other end, as I have sketched here. Sprinkle grated coconut over the top if you want it to be extra special. You should have more fruit salad than the pineapple shells will hold, for they hold very little; but then you can keep the reserve in the refrigerator and refill from it when everyone wants a second helping, as of course they will. And with the mixed fruit juice you may have left over, you could make *kieciel*, page 39, for next day's dessert.

I should add, perhaps, that all the Hawaiian meat dishes I have eaten were accompanied by the most deceptively innocent-looking fruit drinks (in fact, strong rum mixtures), served in a whole pineapple with a straw stuck in its side; this is a pretty and surprising way to serve any summer drink.

CENTRAL AND SOUTH AMERICA

FOUR PYRAMIDS SALAD (from Mexico)   (for 4)

Molé is the classic Mexican way of cooking turkey with chocolate and a lot of other things too. I would not dare to try *Molé* myself, for it is one of the great and complicated secrets of Mexican cooking, and no one but a Mexican, and an inspired cook at that, can do it properly, they say. Nor do I think it would be practical to have a whole turkey with which to experiment. However, I will tell you the story of its origin, as it was told to me in Oaxaca.

Once, long ago, when the Spaniards ruled Mexico, a grandee, the Governor, or Viceroy of New Spain, as Mexico was then known, paid a state visit to the convent of Santa Rosa, for the Sisters were celebrated all over Mexico for their skill in the culinary arts. Sister Andrea was the finest cook in all the convent, and she spent several days trying to invent some wonderful new dish to honour their illustrious guest.

We can imagine the scene when at last she began to cook the dish which was to become famous as *Molé*. The huge kitchen of the convent, with its red-tiled floors, its great open fireplace, framed by blue and yellow tiles; the Sisters all hurrying about, their long sleeves tucked up, stirring, chopping, beating . . . the enormous shining copper pans, the earthenware pots and bowls; the beautiful Mexican peasant girls in their bright skirts, their bare feet pattering across the floor as they fetched water or sliced vegetables, the strong Mexican sunshine beating down outside, and over all the sound of the bells ringing from the old stone belfries, clanging out across the cactus-covered hills, to where the two great volcanoes, Popocatepetl and Ixtacihuatl, stood then as they stand now, unchanging through so many centuries of changing religion and rule.

These are a few of the things Sister Andrea used, making *Molé*. Chilis, the furiously hot little peppers, the *chili chipotle* of Mexico, even hotter than the chili we know here, cloves and sweet pepper and roasted sesame seeds and peanuts, cinnamon, almonds, aniseed, herbs, and some slabs of chocolate, were all ground up together. Then she crushed up garlic, onions, tomatoes, always grinding the different ingredients fine, grinding, grinding, in a brass mortar. Now, grind, or ground, in the Mexican language, is *molé*. Thus, the extraordinary ground-up mixture from which Sister Andrea made a sauce in which to serve her roast turkey came to be the name of her dish. Of course, in addition to all this, the turkey had been fattened for weeks on chestnuts and walnuts, so that it was a particularly sumptuous bird with a very special flavour. After reading all this, you will agree this dish is not for most people to try. I suggest instead Four Pyramids Salad.

This, too, is a typical Mexican dish which takes its name, no doubt, from the great Pyramids of the Sun and the Moon, and others, which rise out of the hills surrounding Mexico City. They are steep, dark, menacing monuments to the Mayan age which is still so much in evidence all over the country.

1 ripe avocado pear	Salt and black pepper, to taste
2 small onions	
2 large ripe tomatoes, peeled	Lemon juice
$\frac{1}{8}$ teaspoon paprika	Lettuce leaves

I know that in England avocados are no longer a luxury. But sometimes one turns out to be over-ripe—not good to eat by itself. Here is a way to use it up.

Take a very ripe avocado; peel it, mash it with 2 small, finely chopped onions and 2 large ripe skinned tomatoes. Add $\frac{1}{8}$ teaspoon paprika and salt and black pepper to taste. When all is well mixed, a squeeze of lemon, and one more rapid stir. Serve it in four neat pyramids, on lettuce leaves (the Mexicans serve it on *tortillas*, flat bread-like slices). Very good as a summer salad.

In Yucatán we were given it rather differently. Four pyramids were served—one of mashed avocado, one of chopped onion, one of small chunks of tomato, and the fourth of a kind of dry grated breadcrumb and goat's milk cheese mixture. Everyone helped himself to as much, or as little of each as he wished. We always wished for several helpings of everything. We used to return to the inn at night, very sharp-set after whole days spent exploring the Mayan temples lying hidden in the green web of the jungle. However early we got up the distances were so great, the jungle so thick, that it was always high noon before we arrived. In the merciless glare, under a brassy sun, we stumbled about the fabulous ruins, each step dislodging an avalanche of rubble and dust to make an archaeologist's mouth water. Sometimes enormous plump iguanas thudded past, galloping, rather than slithering away at our approach. They are harmless creatures—rather taking, I thought—hunted for their meat, which is considered a delicacy for it eats like chicken, they told me in the markets where I saw some of these unhappy iguanas, awaiting the stew-pot. In the markets of Merida, the capital of Yucatán, there is a whole street of booths filled with magic charms and potions, witches' brews, necromancers' philtres, sinister-looking powders, dried bones and skins, recalling the witch-doctors and mumbo-jumbo of black Africa. All over Mexico, the people's sombre attraction for all the symbols and festivals of death are found in the extraordinary variety of sweets and cakes made in the shape of skeletons, coffins, tombstones, and such. Death is always a festival—a release from the bitter business of living, so hard for the paeons. It is quite usual to see a group of beautiful ragged children playing in the dust, under the shade of a giant cactus, their only dolls marzipan skeletons or sugar skulls with liquorice eye-sockets. The babies offer each other especially horrifying symbols of the Crucifixion—Cross, nails, and flails modelled in chocolate or toffee with crowns of thorns in spun sugar, ghastly emblems which they suck with relish, these implacably grave, slit-eyed Mexican babies.

CHILI CON CARNE (from Mexico) (for 4)

This is the national Mexican dish; eaten with *tortillas*, and followed by a slice of papaya, it would be a typical meal, found everywhere, from a restaurant in the big brash port of Vera Cruz on the Gulf of Mexico, to some tiny banana plantation on the Pacific near Tehuantepec, where boa constrictors are used as house pets or mousers— and where the big splendid-looking women stride about in bright yellow, red, and purple costumes, often with little green parakeets sitting on their heads or perched on their shoulders. Most of the men

I saw on the Isthmus of Tehuantepec were dozing in hammocks under the palm trees. Their wives or daughters seemed to be the bosses. In between shouting across the streets to each other and doing the marketing, they were giving the men orders in a very firm way. One old man was making a Chili con Carne. This is how he made it.

1 pound chopped or minced
    steak
1 tablespoon oil
6 ripe tomatoes, chopped
1½ tablespoons chili powder
1 green pepper
1 cup red kidney beans
4 tablespoons water

2 onions, chopped
2 cloves garlic, crushed
Dash of black pepper
¼ teaspoon salt
2 teaspoons flour
1 teaspoon caraway seeds
2 tablespoons cream
    (optional)

One pound of minced steak is broken up well with a fork and browned in 1 tablespoon oil. When seared (about 5 minutes), put it in a big cooking pot that has a lid. Add 6 ripe chopped tomatoes, 1½ tablespoons chili powder, 1 green pepper (seeds removed), cut in strips, 1 cup red kidney beans soaked overnight, 4 tablespoons water. Chop up 2 onions, and fry lightly with 2 cloves garlic, crushed. After 5 minutes add these to the pot; add a dash of black pepper and ¼ teaspoon salt, and see that it cooks very slowly, covered, over an asbestos mat for about 45 minutes at least. Stir it carefully, from time to time. Now take 2 teaspoons flour and I teaspoon caraway seeds, and crush the seeds finely into the flour. Before serving, stir some of the juice from the pot into the flour and caraway mixture, then add it to your stew, and stir well, till it thickens, for about 3 to 4 minutes. At the last moment, some cooks add 2 tablespoons cream, but this is not essential.

This is a rather heavy meal: in Mexico, they would eat it at noon; for supper, probably some *tortillas*, and a cup of chocolate with vanilla whipped into it, if they are well-to-do. In Mexico City, the altitude is such that only very light food is eaten at night. One street celebrated for being the rendezvous of the bullfighters is filled with cafés where they sit with their managers (who look a lot of hatchet-faced thugs), the picadors, and all the hangers-on of the bullring, delicately sipping whipped chocolate, their only sustenance.

THE SAINT'S SAUCE (from Guatemala)   (for 4)

How can one think of food in association with Guatemala, where such an extraordinary, unearthly creature as the quetzal bird actually lives and has its being? This fact alone removes the country into a limbo-land where we seemed to dream we walked . . . where the broken-down buses, which grind a painful (but efficient) way up the mountains, past the turquoise expanses of Lake Aititlan, up, ever up, to hidden highland villages such as Chichicastenango, seem to have no place in this forgotten, magic land.

Here, while the quetzal bird flitters through the forests, with its emerald head and scarlet breast, and long, long green tail plumes, which once formed the Emperor Montezuma's celebrated mantle (now to be seen in a Viennese museum) the Guatemaltéc Indians, Quichés, and Mayans, occupy themselves with strange ceremonies, witchcraft and saint's day processions where Roman Catholic rituals merge with pagan rites, and all night long, deep in the hills, you hear the Indians firing rockets to placate their own special primeval gods.

Poverty is extreme. People eat very frugally. As in Mexico, bread is largely replaced by *tortillas*. The women prepare them at little ovens, on street corners, at the market, and in their own back yards. Everywhere you go, you hear the plip-plop sound of them being patted flat. The sound remains, to me, forever, all of Central America. *Tortillas* require a special sort of corn meal, and take nearly all day to prepare, so I have chosen something easier, and quite as typical, which legend tells, was being cooked at the moment when the terrible earthquake of 1773 destroyed Antigua, the old capital of Guatemala. The convents and churches and palaces of Antigua still remain, beautiful ruins, now covered with masses of tropical flowers; broken fountains still play, and the volcano still towers over the ruins, puffing gently, and the Indians are still crowding into market (held under the huge ruined arches of the Cathedral), and still selling and eating very much what their ancestors did, *tortillas, enchiladas* (a stuffed pancake), beans, pimentos, and coffee or chocolate as a luxury. The sauce I give you is, however, still eaten, among the Spanish rather than Indian population.

This sauce is said to have been found, after the earthquake, unharmed in its little pot, among the ruins of the Governor's Palace; perhaps it is named in reference to the saint who said, 'God walks among the pots and pippins'. It was probably made to eat with some special fresh-water fish from the Lake of Aititlan, but it is excellent with crab, lobster, or, in summer, a cold halibut steak.

1½–2 pounds halibut fillet or any white fish	2 tablespoons yoghourt
6–8 pickled walnuts	Salt, pepper, allspice
¾ cup mayonnaise	1 lemon, quartered
	Watercress (optional)

Poach the halibut fillet in water with ½ teaspoon salt—that is, put the fish in just enough cold water to cover it, bring to the boil, then simmer 10 minutes to the pound. Take it out very carefully, with a spatula. Allow to cool slowly. Serve with Saint's Sauce. For this, get a small jar of pickled walnuts. Mash up 6 or 8, rub through a coarse sieve. Add them to ¾ cup mayonnaise, the ready-made kind will do, and 2 tablespoons yoghourt. Add a little salt and pepper and a pinch of allspice. Whip all together, and serve in a little bowl. Garnish your halibut with quarters of lemon and a plain watercress salad.

HOT-COLD FISH (from Brazil)   (for 4)

Much Brazilian food has a gaudy, brilliant complication, at once exotic and primitive, in keeping with the extraordinary landscape. All round the thrusting skyscrapers of Rio de Janeiro, a great green tide of jungle vegetation surges down from the hills and is scarcely

kept at bay. The vital, primeval forests seem intent on overcoming man's world. Only a few miles into the jungle depths there are monkeys, pumas, snakes, and flashing bright macaws. Up the high reaches of the Amazon where few people penetrate, there are said to be buried temples, treasure, and whole forgotten civilizations waiting to be rediscovered. But I am not tempted when I hear tell of those giant anacondas—serpents 60 and 70 feet long, which lurk in the swamps awaiting their prey, cattle, traders, hunters, explorers —*me*. I know I shall always remain a timid tourist, based in one of the Portuguese baroque towns such as Bahia. And preferably at Carnival time; the fantastic masks and papier-maché monsters will be as near as I shall wish to come to Brazilian fauna. Behind the whole scene, baroque churches, jungles, and the chic night-life of Rio, sounds Gomez music, a sort of tropic opera, where bird-songs, parakeet shrieks, and voodoo drums echo behind the dulcet airs; a counterpoint of sweetness and savagery, echoed too, in the food.

All over South America black beans and rice are staples, to which fiery or surprising ingredients are added. In Brazil, they eat beans with sausages, or pork or a special dried meat. The beans are simmered with onions and tomatoes, and of course garlic. Sometimes chilis and bananas too. The bean and sausage dish is called *feijoada*. Another typical Brazilian dish is *vatapa*, a fish purée with shrimp sauce, not difficult to make, but, like so many foreign recipes, its character and real excellence depend on local ingredients impossible to find elsewhere. However, one typical Brazilian method of preparing fish is easy to do, and can be used for many different kinds. It is a particularly good way to prepare cold fish in hot weather.

1½–2 pounds flat fillets (plaice, sole, haddock)
1 cup white wine vinegar
½ cup salad oil
Salt
Paprika
Peanuts or almonds

Dash of cayenne pepper
2 bay leaves
1 tablespoon tomato purée
2 teaspoons sugar
2 or 3 cloves garlic, crushed
6 medium onions

The fillets are simmered in water to cover for 15 minutes with ½ teaspoon salt, or lightly browned under the grill, and then left to marinate, or soak, overnight, in the following mixture.

Mix together 1 cup white vinegar, ½ cup salad oil, ½ teaspoon salt, dash of pepper, paprika, 2 bay leaves, 1 tablespoon tomato purée, 2 teaspoons of sugar, 2 or 3 crushed cloves of garlic, and about 6 medium onions, peeled and sliced very thin. When the mixture is thoroughly stirred, pour the liquid into a shallow dish and lay the cooked and chilled fillets in it; they should be just covered by the liquid, and the onion rings should be arranged in a thick layer on top. Next day, drain off the liquid and serve the fish cold (with the onions), with a potato and tomato salad and a lavish sprinkling of cayenne pepper and garnished with finely chopped peanuts or almonds first browned in butter. Even the dullest fish will now have acquired a most piquant flavour.

HUANCAINA PAPAS (from Peru) (for 6)

In this wildest, least known, mountainous country of South America they have one speciality which is, I believe, quite unknown elsewhere. This is called *mazamorra morada*, a sort of bright violet-coloured jam, made with a special plant grown only there (and which, logically, should grow in Uruguay, often called the Purple Land, where amethysts abound, even being used, in rough cut chunks, to edge terraces, or flower beds). A more everyday dish much eaten by the Peruvian Indians when they come trudging into market, in their pointed red caps, driving their gentle, furry llamas before them and selling their few wares, baskets, pottery, vegetables, and such, is this *papas*. They picnic by the roadside, eating raw fish from the lakes, with pimento; or *chupe*, a sort of fish soup with egg and cheese and other things added. *Huancaina papas* are not as cannibalistic as they sound, *papas* being potatoes, not parents.

6 large potatoes
1 cup cream cheese
½ cup milk
Juice of 1 lemon
Salt and pepper to taste

1 medium onion or 4 or 5
  spring onions
2 egg yolks hard-boiled and
  mashed
Paprika

Bake 6 large potatoes in a medium oven: about 45 minutes should be long enough. Or you could boil them in water to cover with $\frac{1}{2}$ teaspoon salt for $\frac{1}{2}$ hour. Then peel them and serve them with a sauce made this way: take 1 cup soft cream cheese; beat it up with $\frac{1}{2}$ cup milk, the juice of 1 lemon, salt and pepper, tiny thin shavings of 1 medium onion, or 4 or 5 chopped spring onions (these are best), the mashed yolk of 2 eggs, and a sprinkle of paprika. Serve the sauce either cold or very slightly warmed. Do not let it get hot, or it will be ruined. This would be a good dish for a picnic, as the potatoes could be cooked over the fire and the sauce could be served in a central big bowl, everyone helping themselves.

MOORS AND CHRISTIANS (from Cuba)   (for 4)

In Cuba, country folk eat a dish oddly named Moors and Christians. It is made of black beans and white rice. It is one of the ordinary, everyday dishes of the Cubans, who, when they return at night from their fishing or their work on the sugar plantations, throw themselves down to rest in the wide netted hammocks that stretch from corner to corner of the palm-thatched houses. These, with a table, are often the only furniture they possess. The hammock swinging lazily, outside the door, a little charcoal stove which a child is fanning as the bean stew cooks; a few lean dogs prowling under the tall feathery palms that lose themselves in the starry tropical skies, and a woman lighting a little oil lamp—this is a typical scene in any Cuban village. And this is how to prepare the typical dish they eat for supper.

2 cups lentils or black beans
4 cups water
Salt and pepper to taste
1 large clove garlic, chopped

1 onion
Chopped fresh parsley
Rice (cooked, preferably long-grain)

You must start the night before you want to cook the dish. Take 2 cups black beans if you can get them—if not lentils are good this way, and soak them overnight in 6 cups water. Then next day, about 2 hours before you want to eat them, drain and put them in a pot with 4 cups of fresh water, salt and pepper, 1 large clove garlic chopped very small, and 1 onion, peeled and cut in half. Cover and stew over a low flame for 2 hours or until soft. Drain off the liquid, add a knob of butter and serve with a handful of chopped fresh parsley sprinkled on top and a dish of rice (the long-grain, Patna kind, as for pilaff, page 89, is best).

You might add eggs, and a sauce: tomato or melted butter, or even the sophisticated Sauce Hollandaise—page 170.

THE ZOMBIE'S SECRET (from Haiti) (for 6)

The island of Haiti is full of legends. People will tell you that witch-craft and spells are everywhere. At night, across the palms and tropical gardens surrounding the principal town, Port-au-Prince, you can hear the voodoo drums, strange rhythms, sounds of dancing and singing from faraway villages up the mountainside; it goes on all night, a sinister undertone.

The people talk a graceful, old-fashioned French, dating, perhaps, from the time of the French occupation in the eighteenth century. They will tell you strange stories of Zombies, too. In the old days when the poor slaves died, it was said they were brought back to life by witchcraft. But only a sort of half-life, where they moved about as if in a dream, half awake, working patiently hour after hour. They never spoke and scarcely ate, so they were very cheap slave labour for the unscrupulous plantation owners. (And I must admit I should like to have one in my kitchen, here and now.) They were known as 'Zombies', and legend has it that, since they had no will of their own, they could be made to do anything. Wicked people sometimes used them to perform all sorts of terrible crimes. Although those days have gone, Haiti still remembers its legends, still speaks of Zombies. . . .

One reminder is a dish known in the mountains as the Zombie's Secret. It is said to have been made best by a poor slave, who having died, became a Zombie and was therefore kept making it for every-one, day after day. Then suddenly he disappeared. No one ever found out what happened to him and no one else has ever made it quite so well.

2 avocado pears	1 teaspoon powdered cinnamon
2 bananas	
1 cream cheese, a firm kind	2 tablespoons sugar
2 tablespoons grated coco-nut	½ pint cream
	2 teaspoons very strong coffee or coffee essence

Peel 2 avocados, remove the stones, cut the fruit into chunks about an inch square. Add to them 2 bananas cut into thin rounds, and

1 cream cheese cut in small cubes. Now sprinkle with 2 tablespoons grated coconut and a little powdered cinnamon mixed with sugar (about 3 tablespoons sugar to 1 teaspoon of cinnamon). Chill. Whip $\frac{1}{2}$ pint cream, stir in 2 teaspoons strong sweetened coffee, and pour this over the mixture.

CRÉOLE'S TEMPTATION (from Martinique)   (Party food for 6)

The beautiful tropical island of Martinique is famous for its delectable food and its beautiful women—one of whom was Joséphine Tascher de la Pagerie, she who married Napoleon and later became Empress of France. This particular dish is said to have been one of her favourites, which she introduced to France when everything she said, or did, or wore, or ate set the fashion.

It cannot have been a very slimming food, and when the Empress, who was very vain and took great care of her figure, worked long hours in her beloved garden no doubt she was working off the possible ill-effects of such an indulgence.

2 eggs	1 large lemon
4 bananas	$\frac{1}{2}$ orange
1 cup white breadcrumbs	4 teaspoons butter
$\frac{1}{2}$ cup powdered sugar	1 cup milk

Beat 2 eggs well. Add 4 cut up bananas, 1 cup white breadcrumbs, and $\frac{1}{2}$ cup powdered sugar. Squeeze 1 large lemon and $\frac{1}{2}$ orange, strain the juice, and add it to the rest. Grate into the mixture the rind of $\frac{1}{2}$ lemon. Melt 4 teaspoons butter, add 1 cup milk to them, and put this into the rest. Mash all together with a big spoon.

Butter the inside of a covered mould and sprinkle with powdered sugar. Pour the pudding mixture into it. Put the mould in a large pot half filled with water. If there is more water than that, it may bubble up into the pudding and spoil it.

Heat the oven moderately, put the pot with the mould in it in the oven, and cook for $1\frac{1}{2}$ hours. Look at it from time to time to make sure the water has not boiled away; if it gets very low, add water.

When cooked, lift the mould from the hot-water pot. Dip a knife in the boiling water, then run it around the edge of the pudding to separate it from the mould.

Take the dish on which you want to serve the sweet and put it face down on top of the mould. Hold the two together tightly with the towels and turn them upside down. Then lift the mould off the pudding, tapping the bottom if you need to, to loosen it. Serve warm, and with a thin sauce of either apricot or strawberry jam, to which a little hot water and lemon has been added (I give you directions for a jam sauce on page 16). The Martiniquaise would probably drink rum punch with this, but I think I would prefer a small cup of black coffee, afterwards. In Martinique they might also make their celebrated Café Diable. For this, halve an orange, remove pulp and pips. Put 2 lumps of sugar in, together with a small chopped bay leaf, 2 cloves, a big pinch of nutmeg and another of cinnamon, and a flick of ginger, and two teapoons brandy. Stand a half orange sideways in each cup of strong black coffee. When the coffee soaks through, set light to the brandied sugar. As the flame dies down, tip the whole contents of the orange into the coffee.

THE NORTH

COD'S ROE PIE (from Canada)   (for 4)

The great tracks of the frozen North leading to the Arctic wastes and muskeg country, make one think of the Mounties trailing their man through silent snow-covered forests and occasionally finding time to cook themselves a slice of reindeer or, as a great delicacy, bear's paw. This is the setting of *Maria Chapdelaine*, and *White Fang* and a number of other enthralling novels and movies. On the whole I fancy it is a place I would rather see at a distance from the plush comfort of a cinema seat. With Canada's long coast-line, its great lakes and salmon fisheries, fish is, perhaps, most generally eaten, though pork and beans and pea soup are a standard menu. Here is a recipe for cod's roe as they cook it in Quebec.

1½ pounds fresh cod's roe	1 tablespoon oil
Handful of chopped parsley	1 teaspoon lemon juice
1 cup breadcrumbs	1 cup cooked potatoes, sliced
2 hard-boiled eggs	or mashed (or bread-
Salt and pepper	crumbs)
1 teaspoon anchovy paste	Butter

Boil 1½ pounds fresh cod's roe for about 15 minutes. Skin it, and chop it up in small pieces. Mix it with a handful of fine-chopped parsley, 1 cup breadcrumbs, 2 hard-boiled eggs, chopped, salt and pepper, 1 teaspoon anchovy paste, 1 tablespoon oil, and 1 teaspoon lemon juice. When thoroughly mixed, put in a pie dish or casserole and cover with a layer of cooked potatoes, sliced or mashed, if you have any left-overs. If not, use a thick layer of breadcrumbs, dotted all over with dabs of butter. Bake in a medium oven for about ½ hour.

MOONSHINE (from Iceland)   (for 4)

This silvery dessert seems to belong to the northern snows of Iceland. (Though the only time I was there—between planes—I ate ham and eggs.) I like to think that in this frozen, mysterious northern land there are ice palaces, where beautiful silvery ice princesses are seated on icicle thrones, eating Moonshine. And if there is anything so everyday as a kitchen hidden away in an ice palace (and why not, for there are hot spring geysers which must be very useful in the kitchen), this is how the Moonshine dessert is made.

Powdered gelatine, about 1 ounce
½ cup cold water
2 cups (1 pint) boiling water
6 tablespoons sugar

Rind of 3 lemons, grated
Juice of 2 lemons
2 or 3 egg whites
4 teaspoons sugar

Dissolve 1 ounce of gelatine in ½ cup cold water and let stand for 5 minutes. Add it to a saucepan containing 2 cups, or 1 pint, boiling water, to which is added 6 tablespoons sugar and the grated rind of 3 lemons. Boil all this together for 15 minutes. Put it through a strainer into a bowl; stir in the juice of 2 lemons and let it get nearly cold. Now beat it or whisk it till it is a beautiful snowy white, and rather firm. Put it in the refrigerator till it becomes really firm— 2 or 3 hours—and turn it out like a mould to serve. To garnish, beat the whites of 2 or 3 eggs until very stiff, adding 4 teaspoons sugar. Spread over the dessert.

ESKIMO COFFEE (from Greenland)   (for 4)

This recipe was given me by the man who has been appointed the first Postmaster at the North Pole, which air travel and jet-propelled planes now bring very close. When I made the North Polar flight, from California, by way of Canada, Hudson Bay, and over the great glacier ice-cap of the Arctic (a thirty-hour flight, into Copenhagen), it was of such a transcendental beauty that I was glued to the window, waving aside the series of sustaining meals proffered by the stewardess, being nourished—indeed, positively intoxicated—by the fabulous lunar landscape below. It was high summer; night never fell: the midnight sun glowed on through the small hours, only

sinking to the glittering white horizon to rise again, beside a gigantic crescent moon and one enormous star—Venus—reflected in the turquoise seas and lakes which looked as pellucid as tropic waters. Here, I felt, coral reefs, not icebergs, must abound. In Greenland, Baffin Island, and the few sparsely inhabited islands closest to this arctic zone, the Eskimos are centered in small camp-like villages of huts or igloos; their narrow canoes, *kayaks*, skim the waters in search of fish: for most of the year they wear padded garments and huge fur hoods. The cold is intense, but they still contrive to live rather cosily, I fancy. Walrus steaks, and gulls' eggs are delicacies. There is no pasturage for cows, so there is no milk. I imagine that there, cows assume the same mysterious, unapproachable glamour, as say, Komodo dragons from the Dutch Indies would assume here. The Eskimos trade furs and leather goods for tins of coffee and other rarities. On great occasions (and no doubt the opening of the North

Polar Region Post Office was such), they celebrate with a sort of eggnog coffee, made with gulls' eggs. Try it with ordinary hens' eggs, this way.

4 cups strong black coffee   4–6 tablespoons sugar
4 eggs

Make 1 pot of coffee (4 cups). Meanwhile, beat 4 eggs and about 4–6 tablespoons sugar (this depends on how sweet you like it). Take the coffee off the fire and beat in the eggs quickly. Serve at once, while frothy.

And you could make it an all-Arctic evening by beginning with *Anjovisläda* (page 46) and Moonshine (page 155) to follow.

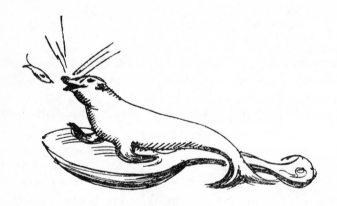

U.S.A.

America is full of the most agreeable regional cooking, from regions as widely different as the Bad Lands, the Deep South (where New Orleans food is world famous), New England, the West—all have their own specialities. Yet the majority of people I met when I was driving across country from New York to Hollywood, by way of Oklahoma, Texas, Colorado, Nevada, and Arizona, which is covering quite a lot of ground, all seemed to be eating the same things—hamburgers, hot-dogs, or ice-cream with monotonous fidelity. Whether they were the rich oil dynasties of Oklahoma, where the derricks and oil-well installations sprout up out of so many back gardens, and fortunes are still made overnight by striking oil, or whether it was the casual motorist like myself, or the cowboys who galloped up Main Street, wherever it was, or even the Navajo Indians—come into town from their Reservations—they all appeared to live off hot-dogs and ice-cream. My first sight of a real Red Indian, like a real cowboy, something I had been awaiting with palpitating heart, was rather a surprise. I arrived in Albuquerque late at night, left my things at one of the motels—these are small brilliantly plumbed bungalows which can be rented by the night, while you leave your car outside, in the manner of a tethered horse. I walked down the straggling neon-lit endless perspective of Main Street to look for my supper. America eats early—dinner, as we know it, is often being eaten at 6 p.m., and is consequently 'off' by 9 o'clock. But that does not prevent you from finding something to eat at all hours, as it does in the English provinces. American drug-stores and snack-bars never seem to shut. Every few yards, between the cinemas, petrol pumps, pin-table booths, and five-and-ten cent stores there were drug-stores or milk-bars, all alike. I turned into one for the excellent reason it was not a darkened cave of uproar consecrated to T.V. Up at the counter sat three huddled figures in blue-jeans. They wore large flat-crowned black hats, and their glossy blue-black hair was tied in long plaits. They were Indians of the Navajo tribe. They sat there, perched on chromium bar stools, sucking ice-cream sodas through a straw. Having been reared on the terrors of early Western films—Black Eagle or Dead Man's Gulch or One Feather Rides Again—these Navajo braves were a disappointment. But then so was my first cowboy. He galloped up out of a cloud of dust on the Arizona horizon, splendidly handsome, standing in the stirrups, his handkerchief scarf fluttering, his spurs jingling ; and tying his pinto pony to the hitching post he loped off down Main Street on those long, incredibly long, legs, their length seeming even more fantastic by the skin-tight frontier pants and high-heeled, foppish, pale-blue boots he wore. So far, he was perfectly true to type. But later I saw him in the drug-store, where everything is bought, from aspirin to lipsticks and hamburgers. He was trying out a new recording of the Brandenburg Concerto and criticizing its orchestration. I turned away sadly, reflecting that real-life America often gives the lie to its movies. Cops are another example of this. We are all familiar with those vigilant, monosyllabic tough guys who dominate crime films. In the flesh—and they are rather a paunchy lot—they are often to be seen sitting up at the drug-store counter, hung about with guns, rounds of ammunition, and nasty looking knives and batons, meekly imbibing a milk shake.

*   *   *

There are, of course, as I said earlier, some magnificent American dishes—and their partiality for adding sweet flavours to meat is at its best in their various ways of cooking ham. This is often basted with sugar, molasses (a kind of treacle) or cooked with peaches or pineapple, and stuck all over with cloves. The sweetness gradually permeates, but very subtly, through the whole ham. This is a reasonably economical meal if you have a large number of people to feed, though whenever I make the initial outlay for such a dish, I shudder, and recall my grandmother's airy dictum: 'Let's buy it now and afford it later.' But for a buffet supper for twenty, say, where the hostess has little time or space to spend in the kitchen, a baked ham is the answer. This is how I used to do it in New York, where my kitchen was about the size of a cabin trunk—hardly large enough for me and the ham to get in together.

BAKED VIRGINIA HAM

1 ham, pre-cooked or other-
    wise
Brown sugar
Sweet vermouth
Powdered mustard

Oranges
Cloves
Pineapple rings or halved
    peaches

If you buy a pre-cooked ham, the cooking time is reduced to a minimum: though I always cooked mine at least 1 hour, in a slow oven, even though pre-cooked. For a ham that is not pre-cooked, reckon 20 minutes to the pound. Thus, a 12 pound ham requires between 3–4 hours. (And feeds about 25–30 people.) Let us assume you have a pre-cooked ham of 7 pounds bought from the grocer, who has skinned it for you. (If not, you must be sure to skin it carefully, yourself.) Put it in a medium oven, without any water, and cook around 1 hour. Now take it out, score the thick outer layer of fat all over in a criss-cross pattern, with a sharp knife. Mix brown sugar, vermouth, mustard, and orange juice or grated orange rind: spread this all over the ham, working it well in. It should be a thick paste. Next, stud the ham all over with whole cloves, sticking them in, one to a criss-cross, so the whole thing looks as if nail-studded. Put it back in the oven with a little extra vermouth or orange juice added to the fat at the bottom of the pan. Leave it in the oven around ¾ to 1 hour basting frequently. The sweet-mustard flavour seeps through the ham, and the outside paste sets, glazes. This lordly dish can be eaten hot or cold. Personally, I think it best tepid— *about the only food that is*—so be sure to take it out of the oven at least 1½ hours before serving, for it cools slowly. In cooling, it firms, cuts easier, and the coating sets into a rich solid outer layer. Some Americans serve pineapple rings round it, or halved peaches—or even glazed cherries. Anyhow, it is a worthy representative of the best American cuisine.

CHEESE-CAKE (from U.S.A.) (for 10)

Americans do not go in greatly for cooked puddings. They are more in favour of their celebrated ice-cream (which eaten with apple pie, they call apple pie à la mode), or a whole series of light fruit and cream whips, or 'ice-box cakes', rich, delicious, uncooked layered affairs that are blended and left to set, or cold-cook, in the refrigerator. Of all their sweets, I prefer cheese-cake, which is the sort of food I imagine one eats in Paradise. At one time, the best brand suddenly went off the market, a clouding piece of news to me, although I was at the moment four thousand miles away from the United States: and I shall always be grateful to an old friend who took the trouble to wire me, when, later, this particular brand of cheese-cake was once more in circulation. Quite soon afterwards, preparing for another journey to America, I wondered what the State Department's response would have been, had I filled up the usual questionnaire: Reasons for requiring an entry permit—quite simply as an 'overwhelming craving to eat So-and-So's cheese-cake'. This delight can be made in various ways—I shall give you a no-bake ice-box way.

2 tablespoons powdered
gelatine
2 eggs, separated
1 cup white sugar
Juice of 4 oranges
3 cups cream cheese

1 cup whipped cream
2 tablespoons melted butter
Pinch of salt
½ cup sweet biscuit crumbs—
shortbread or chocolate

Mix, in a double boiler, ¾ cup sugar, gelatine, pinch of salt. Beat egg yolks and orange juice and add to the gelatine and sugar. Cook all together, slowly (over boiling water) and stir all the while. In about 10 minutes, when it is thickened, remove and allow to cool. Then add the cream cheese, stirring in well. Let it cool till it becomes rather firm. Now beat the egg-whites until stiff, and add the remaining ¼ cup of sugar. Beat the eggs and sugar into the gelatine and cream cheese mixture: add whipped cream. Beat all together vigorously. Put it to cool in a deep cake tin and top with biscuit crumbs that you have first beaten with a little warmed butter. Leave it to 'cook' in the refrigerator. Overnight, if possible. This size cheese-cake should be enough for 10 people—but not nearly enough for me: it is, I think, my favourite food.

EXTRAS

EXTRAS

SIX BASIC SAUCES

Once you know how to make these sauces, you can vary the flavours for whatever you are cooking.

The base of many sauces is called a roux, pronounced 'roo'. It is a mixture of flour with butter. Make it this way: Put 2 tablespoons butter in a saucepan. When hot, add 2 tablespoons flour, stir constantly until it is quite smooth. If you leave it a bit longer, it will turn brown, which may be what you want for your sauce. If you are doing a sauce for meat, it's better brown. Take it off the flame, then add 1 cup liquid, gradually, and stir it thoroughly over low heat until it is thick. Season to taste.

BÉCHAMEL SAUCE is a *roux* made as above with milk, but be sure you do not let the flour and butter brown before you add the milk, for this is a white sauce.

You can add many different things to a Béchamel sauce to turn it into other sauces. If you add 1 tablespoon of grated cheese, you have a cheese sauce. If you add a teaspoon of anchovy essence, you have a sauce for fish. If, instead, you add 1 tablespoon sugar and 1 teaspoon vanilla, you have a sweet sauce to go over desserts: though such a sauce is apt to resemble office paste, to my mind.

Chocolate sauce and some fruit sauces can be obtained ready-made. But if you do have to make them yourself, then there are two easy ways.

CHOCOLATE SAUCE. Melt a bar of chocolate, or 6 tablespoons of cocoa, in 1 tablespoon hot water. Add, bit by bit, more hot water, or warm cream, till you get the thickness and quantity you want. Heat on the fire (low flame), if it's to be served hot. You can add the beaten yolk of an egg if you want it very rich, but take care it does not get too hot, or it will start to cook and turn into a sort of scrambled egg and your sauce will be ruined.

One teaspoon of vanilla flavouring, or rum, is nice in this sauce.

FRUIT SAUCE. The easiest way to make a fruit sauce is to heat ¼ cup good jam with a tablespoon or two of water, and the juice of half a lemon. Apricot, cherry, raspberry . . . all kinds of sauce can be made this way. The lemon juice keeps it from being too sweet.

Or you can cook fruit juice, to which you add almost as much again of sugar, and cook *very* fast, so that it thickens, or reduces, till it becomes a thick sauce.

HONEY SAUCE. This goes well with all fruit salads and many other puddings. Grate the rind of 1 orange and 1 lemon, to make 1 big tablespoonful. Mix this with the juice of both fruits: add this to 1 beaten egg and ½ teacup of light honey: cook over a slow flame (or double-boiler) till it begins to thicken. Allow to cool before serving.

LIGHTNING MAYONNAISE. In general I do not favour kitchen short cuts just for the sake of speed; quality suffers. But here is a way to do mayonnaise without all the usual lengthy ritual.

Take the yolk of one *very* hard-boiled egg (10 mins.), crush it up and add one fresh yolk. With two forks (held in one hand) beat the yolks briskly, together with 4 or 5 tablespoons of oil and some salt and pepper. Keep on turning the mixture, adding a little more oil according to the quantity of sauce required. In a very few minutes your mayonnaise will be ready.

SAUCE HOLLANDAISE. This is especially good to serve with vegetables when they are eaten as a course by themselves: as for example, leeks, cooked cucumber, or cauliflower. In a small saucepan, beat up the yolks of 4 eggs with ¼ cup of cold water. Heat this in a double saucepan, over boiling water: as it begins to warm, and turning all the time, add 4 tablespoons butter, in little pieces, one by one, so that they melt as you stir. When the sauce begins to thicken it is ready. If by chance it appears to curdle, take it off the fire, add a teaspoonful of cold water and go on beating it: it should settle into its smooth thickness again.

GRAVY (for roast meat)

Some unenterprising souls use a ready-made gravy, one that tastes and looks the same for all meat dishes—a thick, dark, uninteresting mess it is, too. The gravy to go with a roast should in each case be made with the fat of the roast and taste of whichever meat it is: veal, lamb, or beef.

After taking the finished roast out of its pan, pour off most of the fat it was cooked in. Leave about 2 or 3 tablespoons in the pan. Into this, sprinkle 1 tablespoon flour, and mix it very thoroughly in the hot fat. When no lumps are left, add 1 cup *cold* water, and cook it all together for a moment or two on top of the stove. Keep stirring, add a little salt and pepper. Your gravy will be rich, dark, delicious, and taste of the roast meat, not just 'gravy'.

* * *

SOME REMARKS ON TEA

Tea is prepared so differently in different countries that it is sometimes almost a thick soup, and sometimes a sort of wine: it all depends where you drink it. Most people we know drink it with milk and sugar, but this would shock the Chinese and Japanese, who are its originators and who drink it in tiny little bowls, very pale-coloured, without either. But in Australia they make it very, very strong, almost black, and stew it all day (that is, the drovers, or cowboys, who drink it out on the range) till it is black as coffee; they take milk if they can get it, and a lot of sugar; I call that tea soup. The Russians and Poles drink tea in glasses, often with a slice of lemon in it, and keep watering it down from a samovar, or tea-urn of boiling water. They like to add a spoonful of jam. The old-fashioned peasants I knew used to drink it through a lump of sugar they held in their teeth, sucking it in noisily to express their satisfaction. In Tibet, they add chunks of yak fat or butter.

In the Argentine they drink a special kind of *maté* tea, made from a strong herb; this is the favourite drink of the *gauchos*, or cowboys of Argentina. In France, people drink very little tea, preferring coffee. If you offer them tea, they will often say, 'No thanks, I'm not ill'—meaning that they only drink tea as a medicine—for a bad cold, perhaps. But they do drink *tisanes*, which are a sort of herb tea, differently flavoured: peppermint, camomile, and so on. They are supposed to be good for the digestion, and you often see a French family who have been seated at the table for several hours eating a splendid dinner of five or six different courses: soup, fish, meat, salad, cheese, dessert, coffee, and wines, all asking most anxiously for a *tisane*. Perhaps it is just as well after such a large meal.

The English are the people who, most of all, enjoy their cup of tea. To London, the tea-urn is as symbolic of the city as are the fountains of Berne, or those little kiosque *pissoirs* of Paris. Sporting events and social triumphs are both punctuated by cups of tea; the tea-urn, in varying degrees of electro-platedness or gold-platedness is found at both the Derby and Buckingham Palace Garden Parties. Theatre intervals provide occasion to rush to the bar, where, surprisingly, the tea-urn does a brisk trade; and matinées are made hideous by the distribution of tea-trays, which always arrive just as the curtain goes up, and have to be passed along with much whispering, apologies, and rattling of change. Actors accept the fact they must speak above the clink of the teacups; but then they are well-trained, for English comedies abound in tea-table scenes where the whole ritual is followed faithfully, 'One lump or two? Milk? Lemon? Just *one* more cup then. . . .'—this passing for dialogue.

There are two sorts of tea most generally used, although there are all kinds of sub-divisions. China tea is very subtle in flavour. Indian tea is more emphatic. It is all a matter of what you like; either kind is seldom well made, I find. The water *must* boil; one spoonful of tea for each person, and one for the pot is the old rule. It should not go on stewing, but be drunk at once. The addition of a little lemon or orange peel, cut very thin, dried, and left in the package of tea (which must be kept in an airtight tin, by the way) adds a lovely, strange, and delicate flavour—though a good tea should be lovely and strange and delicate enough in itself.

Remember, when you wash up, don't throw the tea leaves down the drain. They block it and give it a lot of trouble.

And on this sober, utilitarian note, it seems appropriate to end. For most of us, the problem of plumbing still clouds the joys of cooking. Choked sinks, bulged dustbins, and the horrors of waste-disposal in old-fashioned houses and converted flats—these things leave their mark. When people ask me what I most enjoyed doing in New York I have my answer ready; using those built-in rubbish chutes that are found in most well-equipped kitchens. One flick of the wrist, and potato peeling, empty jars, paper bags, bones . . . all the unmanageable mountains of débris that accumulate are instantly swallowed in its ever-gaping maw. (I used rather to envy the mediaeval way so many less civic-minded New Yorkers did not hesitate to throw their rubbish out in the gutter, without the least scruple, making their city one of the dirtiest I have ever seen, but displaying, also, a sort of *après moi le deluge* insouciance I found very refreshing.

But what have these sordid details to do with good cooking? They are mere mechanics, I hear you say. By which I know you have not been cooking long. In the kitchen, no mechanics are mere. The finest flights of fancy are clouded by the business of clearing up. As the Frenchman said when he presented his lady-love with a refrigerator, rather than pearls: "One needs a solid base for one's follies."

A POSTSCRIPT

If you are making your début in the kitchen, remember that there is as much art in putting a menu together, planning a meal, as in the cooking. Useless to make a splendid soup, follow it by a gravyfied ragout, and a compôte. The whole stomach is awash.

Not only substances, but textures and colours, like flavours, must vary—must set each other off. Don't, for instance, start off with tomato soup if you are going to have salmon; it's all so pink. Don't begin a meal with a cheese soufflé if you have decided on a fruit fool for your dessert. Perhaps the most difficult dishes to accommodate are the sumptuous suet puddings; they *will* take pride of place; *will* dominate, by sheer majesty and bulk, the rest of the menu. They should, to my mind, be treated as the *pièce de résistance*, and prefaced accordingly, by something simple, grilled fish, or a roast chicken; a salad as a course by itself—and then, the pudding. I recommend reading and collecting cook-books, as varied as possible, from the health-food nut-cutlets school to Mrs. Beeton's gargantuan spreads. They give one a lead, and are always among my favourite bedside books. And Ali, a Tunisian cook (who could neither read or write) was always poring over my collection. *They inspire me*, he said.

I hope my book will do likewise, for you.